CHANGING

— WITH —

FAITH

WORDS OF ENCOURAGEMENT

JOYCE
AND
GARY THIBO

WESTBOW
P R E S S®
A DIVISION OF THOMAS NELSON
& ZONDERVAN

WestBow Press books may be ordered through booksellers or by contacting:

WestBow Press
A Division of Thomas Nelson & Zondervan
1663 Liberty Drive
Bloomington, IN 47403
www.westbowpress.com
1 (866) 928-1240

ISBN: 978-1-5127-0480-8 (sc)
ISBN: 978-1-5127-0479-2 (e)

Library of Congress Control Number: 2015911706

Print information available on the last page.

WestBow Press rev. date: 8/25/2015

Therefore whoever hears these sayings of Mine, and does them, I will liken him to a wise man who built his house on the rock. Matthew 7:24 NKJV

In a rapidly changing world the one thing that stays the same is God. He is the same yesterday, today and tomorrow. Reading people's writings of Christian encouragement and guidance can place us on the course of real change. The Bible is the foundation of change and God's word is the bedrock that foundation is built on. Today the ideas of man are so often built on shifting sand. That shifting sand is fame, wealth and power and when shaken these ideas can fall into ruin.

God's word can build a strong foundation where people can prosper and become a success. To be truly successful you have to obey the word of God. Jesus used the example of the shifting sand but few people today heed His warning. In this changing world all Christians need to focus on the word of God to guide their lives to success. The bedrock of faith in God provides a strong foundation. That foundation is the word of the risen Lord Jesus Christ.

Many today want to do more, reaching out to those in need. We can only hope that these writings gave you the encouragement you need. Bible study and prayer are most important, but reaching out to those who do not know the Lord is when real success begins to happen. Many who read this are already on that journey of change, we can only hope you will inspire more people to join in your efforts.

If you took time to read our words of encouragement we thank you from the bottom of our hearts, for blessing us with your interest. We are praying that you will make a meaningful change in the lives of all you meet on your walk with Christ.

Thank you,
Joyce and Gary Thibo

Writing personal messages to people that have suffered with drug and alcohol problems started us writing the message we give today. Christians need to reach out more to all they meet. This sounds simple but many do not talk frankly about their faith in the Lord. Going about our daily tasks we encounter many troubled people that don't know the Lord. Work is a place where you can share your faith with many troubled souls that need the word of the Lord. Even at church you can reach out to members that are now experiencing problems that you have had in your own life.

Reaching out to youth is very important and helping them cope with problems that you had to work through can be a blessing to them. Many churches in our area have an older membership and if we don't reach out to the youth, many churches will not survive. To make a better tomorrow, we need to put our focus on the needs of young people today. We need to tell them about the blessing of having the word of God in their life.

Financially sound teaching is also important and we encourage helping individuals with gifts of money and goods. The word of God coupled with a monetary gift can help a person to examine their life. Getting people to think about what God wants in their life is the basis of real change. Putting God first is the most important lesson that can be learned.

After writing hundreds of messages to people that have changed our lives, we would like to share some of our writings *that we hope will help you to reach out to those who do not know the risen Lord Jesus Christ.*

We hope that you find at least one message that is useful to you on your walk with Jesus.

Lord help all who read this message to reach out to those that don't know the Lord.

*A*ny concern to small to be turned into a prayer is to small to be turned into a burden. *Corrie Ten Boom*

Every day people worry, but like they say if you have time to worry you have time to pray. People that don't know the blessing of God feel overwhelmed by problems of everyday life. Prayer can clear your mind of problems and fill your heart with determination.

God's word is like a compass guiding you on the path of life. For those that don't know the Lord confusion and inaction can cause a myriad of problems. God's word can calm the most troubled person and your caring and love can help them come to know the Lord.

Worry is not trusting God and that is a sin. Now that's something to worry about. Many today don't trust God to handle problems. Ask God to help you not to worry. Trust Him to provide a calm spirit to come into your heart. God will give you the strength to solve the most complex and confusing situations. Ask God to forgive you for worrying and ask Him to take away anything that is distressing you.

Health, finance and family problems can cause us to be anxious. When we worry it is a sign that we are not completely trusting God. Trust God completely to help you to resolve the problems you are facing. Turn to the word of God for wisdom and turn to prayer for guidance. No matter how difficult a problem there is no need to worry. God is there to guide you in all decisions great or small.

Lord, how can I worry with you by my side, thank you for coming into my life and guiding me on Your path.

The secret of the Lord is with those who fear Him, And He will show them His covenant. My eyes are ever toward the Lord, For He shall pluck my feet out of the net. Psalm 25:14-15 NKJV

Our outward appearance is like the snow hiding a multitude of sins. As I look out on the field next to my home the beauty of the fresh snow makes me forget what is really there. The beautiful snow covered field is really piles of dirt, rocks and rubble left from a failed construction site. Snow covers the worst scenery and makes it look beautiful.

Our lives can be just like that construction site. Troubles of all sorts can distress us as we put on the appearance that nothing is wrong. That's human nature, putting on a front to keep people from knowing you have problems. For some people the problem their trying to cover up is sin. They may be doing something dishonest or self destructive all the while presenting a Christian image. Just like snow on a field it is hard to see what is underneath.

My mother would look out at our backyard which was really a junkyard and say snow covers a multitude of sins. If your life is filled with the junk of life, the sins of man, ask God to help. Honesty is what God wants. He wants you to put down those things that you know are wrong.

Are you hiding some junk in your life that needs to be removed? Ask God to come into your heart and wash it white as snow.

"Show me your ways, Oh Lord; Teach me your paths."
Psalms 25:4 NKJV

Lord, make me a green pasture and a straight path for all those who need your word.

When I feel hurt or broken hearted God binds up my wounds and cures my pain and sorrow. Psalm 147:3 AMP

The E.M.T.'s respond to all sorts of accidents and crimes. The injured person's life is the number one priority. It doesn't matter whether they're rich or poor. It doesn't matter if they were involved in a crime or tried to kill themselves. The E.M.T. is there to save that person's life. If you believe in God your life has been saved. You will live forever because of your faith in the risen Lord Jesus Christ. The earthly suffering we face now will fade away as our new life in heaven begins.

The power of man is limited when it comes to saving a person's life. No matter how skilled the emergency medical tech is God has the final say. There is nothing sadder than seeing a young person lose their life. There is nothing more confusing than seeing a violent criminal being resuscitated. People that see a lot of life and death situations often have a very different perspective about God's will. We don't know how God works in other people's lives, but we do know how He works in ours, encouraging us to reach out to others. That is what an E.M.T. does, they reach out to save the lives of people they don't even know.

As Christians we need to reach out to those who are not saved and not judge people by their past. Like the E.M.T., we should want to save everyone because of their need.

Are you coming to a loved ones rescue before it is to late? Are you reaching out to those who need assistance no matter how checkered their past.

Lord, Give me the power to respond to an emergency and take away the fear from my heart.

For we walk by faith not by sight. 2 Corinthians 5:7 NKJV

Walking in the footsteps of someone who has walked before you makes it easier to get through the snow and slush. Placing your foot in some other adventurous person's footprint can make your walk simpler and less tiring. The only thing you have to watch out for is where that other person may have fallen. The winters here can be quite treacherous because of deep and slushy snow. Heavy snow can hide all sorts of junk that you can fall on and get hurt. Life can have unseen junk; the Bible calls them stumbling blocks.

These stumbling blocks are the junk that causes pain, heartache and depression. This junk causes a stumbling block that produces a nasty fall. If you're walking in Jesus' footsteps, these problems won't cause a stumbling block. God's word alerts you to problems that are arising in your life and through prayer you can work through these difficulties that are caused by all the unseen junk. The Bible states that through the power of the risen Lord your life will be guided by the Holy Spirit. When problems arise you are given the power to get through any situation. All you have to do is have faith in God.

Is the Holy Spirit guiding you on your dangerous walk through the stumbling blocks of life? Do you trust the footprints that you walk in today? If not, ask Jesus Christ into your heart to guide you through the stumbling blocks of life.

Lord, make my way clear; free from stumbling blocks so I can travel this snowy road to help those less fortunate than me.

A nd the prayer of faith will save the sick, and the Lord will raise him up. And if he has committed sins he will be forgiven. Confess your trespasses to one another, and pray for one another, that you may be healed. James 5; 15-16 NKJV

We are jars of clay, formed by the Creator. Many of us are broken and cracked, but the light of God shines out from those cracked and broken jars. That's what helping and caring for others is about. No matter what trauma or pain you have suffered in your life, the light of God can still flow from you. James says to draw near to God and He will draw near to you.

You can only draw near to God through prayer. These times of prayer are quiet time, of just your thoughts and the power of God bringing about change. These times of prayer are what will reform your life and help you encourage others. God is the potter you are the clay. The light that shines within you is the faith and wisdom that God has granted to you, don't let it go to waste. Seek out others that could use your help through the word of God.

God formed us as a potter forms a clay vessel, but along the way we become damaged and maybe broken. His words can fix the most damaged and broken vessel all you have to do is truly believe. Once God has filled your heart with His Holy Spirit a light will shine from within you. Like a light shining from inside a broken jar we are able to reach out to others. With God's word giving you wisdom, you will be a beacon of light to other lost souls.

Are you reaching out to others that are broken or damaged?

Lord help all of us to use our wisdom to spread your word to all those people that have not seen your light.

*B*eloved, I pray that you may prosper in all things and be in health, just as your soul prospers. For I rejoice greatly when brethren came and testified of the truth that is in you, just as you walk in the truth. I have no greater joy than to hear that my children walk in truth. 3 John 4 NKJV

A parent can have no greater joy than to know their children walk in the truth. A man told of how he had used drugs and alcohol and still advised his children to abstain from these things. He finally realized the error of his way and put down these pleasures of man. He said how could he advise against something he did. You have to set an example for your family.

John writes to encourage new believers But those who have come to know the Lord a long time ago need to lead and guide the new converts to Christianity. Take time out to read 3 John, you will see people are encouraged to put away the ideas of the past and follow the teachings of the Risen Lord. To set a course of change for the betterment of mankind. To help prepare others for the journey. That journey is their walk in the truth.

We are concerned with our children and how they transition to adulthood. If they know the word of God they are far better off when troubles come into their lives. Walking with God is a lifetime journey that gives us wisdom. The sooner we start our children on the path of knowledge in the word of God, the better they will be prepared for the demands of life.

Are you encouraging your children to take part in the word of God and the fellowship of a Bible based church?

Lord, help my children draw closer to you.

*W*hen the righteous cry for help, the Lord hears and delivers them out of their troubles. The Lord is near to the brokenhearted and saves the crushed in spirit. Psalm 34:17-18 ESV

Grief is like a shadow cast upon your life. The example of a bus passing by you on a street and casting a shadow on you comes to mind. You weren't hit by the bus but you were covered by the shadow. The sad part is, many that are covered by the shadow wish that they were hit by the bus.

A lot of times I see an older man who has lost his wife fall into a state of confusion from grief sometimes becoming very depressed. Older women experience the same thing but seem to hide it better. The idea of the strong family patriarch seems to be the reason. The strong mother figure that can solve problems gives the illusion that grief is not influencing their life. This can cause depression to creep into their lives and cause all sorts of trouble.

While working at an older woman's house she began to tell me about how her knees were bothering her and that the pain was causing her great frustration. I told her we would pray for her and I encouraged her to do the same. Over time I realized that the death of her daughter was the root cause of her pain. But God was in her life and one day at church she came up to me and told me she had sought counseling for her depression. The last time I talked to her she was back on track and things were looking up. God has a way of fixing things all you have to do is admit you have a problem and *ask him to help you. Through prayer and his grace you will be healed.*

Are you feeling depressed because of the loss of a loved one? Seek out one of the many groups that counsel those suffering from grief related depression.

Lord, lift this heavy burden from me so I can be a more valuable servant.

" *Therefore do not worry saying," "What shall I eat?" or "What shall I drink?" or "What shall I wear?"*
Matthew 6:31 NKJV

One day at a time has been a popular phrase for many years. Jesus used this idea to reassure his disciples that God had control over their life and that the things of man really didn't matter. Today so many take pride in their possessions and their wealth yet still feel anxious and depressed. Anxiety overcomes many in the quest for success, but many of these people are not walking the path with God.

Money, power and pleasure can all be God given. Sadly those that store up treasures on earth are traveling down a path that does not lead to the kingdom of God. God wants the best for you, but many times we think that it involves money and status. Today our society has turned toward the concept of how to monetize almost everything. It's all about making a buck. Still many focus on the real meaning of life, that is true faith in God. When you come to know God, problems melt away like snow on a warm spring day. Our life becomes filled with beauty and refreshed by joy. Like the first green grass and the wild flowers of spring our life is renewed with the loving word of God.

Looking at the verse above I found it odd that my life had been changed by this simple sentence. One day at a time is what trusting God is really all about. It's not about all the things that man has made. Life is about the promise of a better tomorrow through your faith in the power of God.

Are you trusting God to improve your life? Are you trusting in Him to guide you on the path to success?

Lord, help me have a successful life, one that is rooted in your word.

*T*herefore I tell you, Whatever you ask in prayer, believe that you have received it, and it will be yours. Mark 11:24 ESV

The rule of one fifty is the Dunbar principle. Anthropologist Robin Dunbar first proposed that brain size and long term memory limit us to relationships with around one hundred and fifty people. This is a problem at large churches and big companies alike. Some people feel they don't get the attention they deserve and they may be right according to the rule of one fifty. Numbers vary with groups and organizations but most of the time people don't get the attention they expect when the numbers get to high.

For me that happens at about fifteen people. I confuse names, job titles and just make a fool of myself in general. My desire to inform and help people for me is better done one on one. That's how it is with God. He works one on one with you to lead and guide you to a better life. We all have our shortcomings. The quicker you recognize those shortcomings the faster you can improve your ability to reach out to others.

People tell you problems that may seem to hard to solve but the word of God can calm the most troubled person. Be honest and tell those people that you have never experienced the problem they're having. Kindness is important in all your conversations but sincerity is key. So many that listen to people's problems don't care and that isn't helpful. Be honest if you don't think you can help.

Tell the person upfront that you don't think your qualified to help solve their problem. The person who listens with an *apathetic ear can cause confusion and distrust. Reaching out to help is not for everyone. If God has truly put this on your heart you need to be effective, caring and helpful. Learning to help people can be challenging, but it will help make you the person you've always wanted to be, more like Christ.*

N*ever be afraid to trust an unknown future to a known God." Corrie Ten Boom.*

When we doubt with our mind, desire with our hearts and disobey with our will is when evil overcomes us. Only the power of God can break us free from the grip of evil. To change and become a better person is a message conveyed from Genesis on in the Bible.

The New Testament tells us to be Christ like. For those that have lived in both worlds, good and evil, choosing God has inspired them to reach out to others. Many people that have faced personal hardships, substance abuse and financial turmoil ask God for help. The power of God can change the most troubled life and those who receive that gift feel compelled to reach out to others in need.

A good friend of mine passed away last week and he had lived in both worlds. Once he came to know the Lord the things of the past became a distant memory. He had no desire to turn back to the path of lies and regrets. He had no desire to revisit his life before Christ came into his heart. He did have a strong desire to rescue those that had strayed off course. Those who doubted with their mind, desired with their heart and disobeyed with their will.

Guiding family, friends and strangers to see the love and comfort in God's word was a full time job for my friend. We are saved by God from ourselves and with our new found freedom we feel compelled to reach out to those in need.

Are you reaching out to those that need the word of God? Are your talents and wisdom being used to improve the lives of those around you?

Lord, clear the path for those that travel on it to hear Your word.

*T*he fruit of the righteous is the tree of life; and he that winneth souls is wise. Proverbs 11:30 KJV

You know what is nice? When you're asleep and your wife reaches out putting her arm around you. She draws near to you and a comforting feeling that you are loved comes over you. God is like that; he draws close, to give you comfort and solace. Many though don't turn to God in times of need. They rely on the word of man and the distractions of everyday life for comfort.

People over estimate a person's power to make their lives better. Someone who has lost a loved one or suffered through a divorce needs all the help they can get to put their life back on track. God's word and quiet time in prayer can help you to return to a normal life. Also good Christian friends can provide that special care needed to get you through those difficult times.

Many don't look at all the blessing they have had in their lives. Jobs, education and family is what makes life worth living. Sadly many Christians feel separated from God. People feel overwhelmed by their jobs, burdened by the cost of their education and disappointed with their family. Just the fact that they have come to know Jesus is a blessing that can't be measured. God is there for you and wants you to draw nearer to Him. If you do this you will know that you are truly loved.

Are you drawing closer to God for comfort and solace? Or are you looking to the words of man to help you with the distractions of life?

Lord help me draw closer to you, avoiding the distractions of man.

*A*nd do not be conformed to this world, but be transformed by the renewing of your mind, that you may prove what is that good and acceptable and perfect will of God. Romans 12:2 NKJV

To know the word of God and apply it to our everyday life isn't an easy task. My wife speaks about how you can come to know the Lord. You must put down the past and change your heart and mind. She teaches about walking with God and asking Him for guidance. In our everyday lives, personal problems, politics, financial status and our own brand of religion turn us against people we're trying to help. These prejudices are what keep us from doing real constructive work.

Christ's love in our hearts lets us forgive all people. Our own petty jealousy, egos and personal problems may cause us to not show the love of God to our fellow man. Strong opinions, short tempers and problems over money often cause us to become involved with behavior which God does not approve. Each day we must strive to improve our lives to be better Christians.

Turn your heart away from the old and focus on the new. The true love of God will be the force of change in your life. Truly walking with God is all about a journey of change and learning. This adventurous quest will change your heart and mind, making you the person God wants you to be. Whether you have just started or are well on your way God is by your side in the journey of change.

Many today are afraid to step out on their own to make a change in their life, but God is right by your side. If you have problems, all you have to do is sincerely ask him to lead and guide you.

Lord, give me the strength to focus on you for change.

"*And He said to her, Daughter, be of good cheer, your faith has made you well. Go in Peace. Luke 9:48 NKJV*

The Holy Spirit flows freely from God to those who are deserving. The women with an issue of blood is an example of this. Through her faith all she had to do was touch Jesus' robe. The power came out of him and healed her. He tells her to go in good cheer. Not to many physicians use that as a closing statement today. The sad part is many people don't need a physicians help they need God's word.

Today all we have to do is pray to God and he heals us. Worry and doubt have separated us from God. We all know we can't live forever that is why it is important to respect the body God has given us. The wisdom we glean from our own troubles can be the knowledge that helps us help others. To help a troubled person it takes the eyes of a person who has seen troubles. To comfort the ill it takes those that have seen illness themselves. God gives us wisdom though our life experiences to not only improve our lives but the lives of others.

Be of good cheer is what Jesus tells the woman with the issue of blood, after she is healed. People need to remember that phrase. Today we hear stories of pain and suffering with very little discussion about the blessings God has given to his faithful. Your faith will make you well. You still may have a limp and a sore back but you should be of good cheer. Today we would call that an attitude of gratitude.

Do you have an attitude of gratitude? Are you showing good cheer because of your faith in God?

Lord, you have shown me your love and I will be thankful.

*P*eople often forget that the Psalms were set to music.
For the chief musician. A Psalm of David.

Oh Lord you have searched me and know me. You know my sitting down and my rising up; You understand my thought far off. You comprehend my path and my lying down, And are acquainted with all my ways. Psalm 139:1-3 NKJV

In the past few months I have decided that before I die I would like to learn something new. At a Goodwill store I came across a nice electric guitar and took it to a local musician that did repairs. He had it sounding great in about a day, I'll probably spend the rest of my life, trying to make it sound good.

When it comes to the people we meet in our lives, some far excel our abilities and display a talent that we can never achieve. But this should not dissuade us from trying our best and pursuing our dreams. You should never stop learning is the old self help motto. Life is full of opportunities to learn and gain wisdom. Everyone should spend some time learning something new. To explore new ideas and broaden our horizon instead of sitting around broadening our rear ends.

Today there are so many ways to improve your education, knowledge and wisdom. My wife and I give a message that is based on the study of the Bible and reaching out to those that don't know the Lord. People that are involved in music seem to be friendly and helpful with a general concern for the betterment of others. In the few weeks of trying to learn to play, people have shown me all sorts of basic ideas, on how to improve my skills. Some people even invited me to try to play along with them knowing my limited ability. Leaving a store I told a friend I wish I would meet Christians who show the same enthusiasm as people involved in the music field. Most have been kind and caring not concerned about money and eager to have you learn something new.

or am I now seeking the approval of man, or God? Or am I trying to please man? If I were still trying to please man, I would not be a servant of God. Galatians 1:10 ESV

The ability to change people's minds is a gift. But the power to change their hearts is a gift from God. Many people speak to groups in the hopes of swaying opinions for or against a certain cause that they are promoting. But many people have a greater good in mind, to change a person's heart. To tell people of a higher power that is life changing.

It is this power of God that will cure all problems and calm the most confused mind. Many face troubles today that are hard if not impossible for some people to overcome. Complete faith in the Lord is how change is put into action. This is the change of heart that gives you the power to forgive. This faith in God is what will allow you to regain control of your life and overcome your problems.

My wife is speaking tonight with the hopes of changing people's minds. The talk will focus on leaving the past behind and walking in a new life with Christ. Those that accept this challenge will have a change of heart that is brought about by their faith in the Lord. Sadly many will miss out on this opportunity because of their love of the pleasures of man.

To turn away from the things that man so dearly loves is not an easy task. To make people want to lay down the things of man that will cause them pain and suffering is hard to achieve. It can only be done with prayer and the power of God's word. I can only hope that through the power of God, my wife's message will cause people to come to know the Lord so they will have a change of heart.

Lord, help us to show people what is really important, faith in Your word and Your power to change a person's life.

" *Do they not provoke Me to anger?" says the Lord. "Do they not provoke themselves, to the shame of their own faces?" Jeremiah 7:19 NKJV*

Writing something that will turn people away from drugs is not an impossible task. Most people that live in the world of substance abuse turn away when they become too tired to continue. For some, substance abuse is like a shovel, all they do is end up digging their own grave. Only faith in the Lord can give you the strength to overcome drugs and alcohol. For many when they are at their lowest is when God came into their heart. Tired and weary, broken and confused many former revelers at the all-night pursuit of pleasure ask God to save them from themselves.

If you're tired and weary choose the life giving water that is faith in Jesus Christ. Leave substance abuse in the past and travel the road to the Kingdom of Heaven.

Have you become tired of your lifestyle? Are drugs and alcohol ruling your life? Are you ashamed when you look in the mirror? Are you tired of digging your own grave? Stop digging and lay down your shovel. Turn to the word of God to help you out of the pit you have dug for yourself.

"Call to Me and I will answer you, and show you great and mighty things, which you do not know." Jeremiah 33:3 NKJV

Lord open up the hearts and minds of those who are enslaved to drugs so your word can free them from their chains.

"*But if you love those who love you what credit is that to you? For even sinners love those that love them. And if you do good to those who do good to you what credit is it to you? For even sinners do the same.*" *Luke 6:32 NKJV*

Reflecting on her past a young girl whose life was one of poverty and despair remembers the kindness that was shown to her at vacation Bible school. She vows to turn her life around and goes on to be an inspirational leader at a local church. A young woman battling substance abuse who had heard the word of God as a child reaches the lowest rung of the ladder and asks God to save her from herself. Today, fully recovered, she guides others to come to know the Lord. Having lost her way on the road of life a former biker chick, as she would say, goes from one abusive relationship to the next looking for love. Depressed and confused she remembers the enthusiasm she had while working with a church group years ago. Today she has found love in God's word and works with abused women helping them rebuild their lives.

Most church goers have a favorite story or childhood memory about an inspirational person that changed their life. For some it's the memory of singing or a mission trip with a youth pastor that made a difference in their life. The important words are, made a difference, for when I hear stories about those words, it is the difference between life and death. Are you making a positive impression on the youth at your church? Are you making a difference?

Lord, help me to encourage others to reach out to the young people they know, providing a positive role model for them by using Your word.

*D*o not be conformed to this world, but be transformed by the renewing of your mind that you may prove what is that good and acceptable and perfect will of God. Romans 12:2 NKJV

Ask not what people can do for you ask what you can do for people. This is an idea of what God wants for mankind. In the early sixties president J.F.K. used a similar phrase that was from a Hubert Humphrey speech. It was the marching orders of a generation of change. Today we need change and improvement in our complex world. Both sayings should be close to your heart.

A large growing population having to personally interact less with people and more with technology has made many distant and uncaring. History, religion and philosophy are taught in the university but are not being integrated into popular culture. Most people know more about technology than history. There is an old saying, those that do not know history are doomed to repeat it. In the years that have past since J.F.K. was killed we have slipped into a mindset that the past doesn't matter. But many of the problems we face today are as old as the Bible.

Just now, as churches are facing changes to leadership the foundation of real change needs to be built. Changing to the younger generation is a blessing and will help us become more concerned about how people can be helped. Christianity in many areas of this country has lost membership and core members are over fifty. This is not just an aging baby boomer problem it is a problem of what the church has to offer. If *your church is in need of an overhaul or you are in the process of transitioning to a younger group of leaders it is important to focus on building a good foundation. One of outreach to the community and needy.*

Do you have a plan for change and transformation?

Lord, put our fellow man's needs in our hearts so we can be a beacon of light to them in a storm.

" *For God did not send His Son into the world to condemn the world, but that the world through Him might be saved." John 3:17 NKJV*

God has a plan for your life. When you were born, God had a plan for you. No person has to worry, all they have to do is follow what God wants for them. Sadly for many people, God is asking them to change but they refuse. They fight and struggle against the word of God and their life is filled with problems. The hard parts of life can be what brings us closer to God.

Lives are wasted every day in the pursuit of pleasure. Many use drugs and alcohol in a vain attempt of finding happiness. Those revelers at the all night pursuit of pleasure end up traveling on the road to ruin. Many who travel this road find it only leads to an early grave. Lying to others and to themselves, people that are controlled by substance abuse become mired in the mud that leads to their ruin. Fortunately some will gain a foothold and find a path to recovery. Many though will only find suffering, unhappiness and death, this may sound harsh but it is true.

God never leaves these people lives. He is always there waiting for them to ask sincerely for His help. All you have to do is ask God into your heart and lay down the pleasures of man. Through your prayers to God the Holy Spirit will guide your life back to a calm state of normality. This doesn't happen overnight because most of us fight against change; seeking the pleasures that caused our demise. Still once you have truly asked God into your heart there is a change. The

Spirit of God will lead and guide you to a new life, one without the need for drugs and alcohol.

Lord help me guide others to the path that you have made for those that are lost. Let me be a beacon of light on the path of recovery so those lost souls can find You.

*M*y people have done two evil things: They have forsaken me, the Fountain of Life-giving Water; and they have built for themselves broken cisterns that can't hold water! Why has Israel become a nation of slaves? Why is she captured and led far away? Jeremiah 2:13-14 TLB

So often we over promise and under produce. Not just in our walk with Christ but in every aspect of our life. This is where personal honesty comes into play. Many set out to change the world but don't think about changing themselves. We could all use a makeover but some need a complete rebuild. The word of God can repurpose your life. A complete renewal of spirit and a transformation of heart and mind.

Life-giving Water is what provides change. It is offered freely to all that are willing to follow the word of God. To those brave enough to take a different path than those that pursue the pleasures of man. Drinking the Life-giving Water of God's word provides change and a feeling of joy that can't be found anywhere else. Like Jesus told the woman at the well "if you drink of this water you will never thirst."

Today people everywhere have become enslaved to the pleasures of man. Drugs alcohol and promiscuous sex rule many lives. If you are one of those people that feel enslaved to the pleasures of man there is hope in the word of God. Through the Life-giving Water of God's word you can have real joy and happiness.

Is your thirst being quenched by the Life-giving Water? Are you questioning why you're seeking the pleasures of man?

Lord, Help me find my way to the Life-giving Water that is the word of God.

" *A* nd the King will answer and say to them, Assuredly, I say to you, inasmuch as you did it to one of the least of these My brethren, you did it to Me". Matthew 25:40 NKJV

Most people are wealthy until they have to open their wallets to give money. Give is the keyword. When asked to give many people's net worth suddenly is cut in half. Most people will gladly lend or invest, but when it comes to giving, things change. Today many are in need. Also many churches need repairs and improvements. Trusting God is just that, if you believe your giving goes to God's work you can't go wrong. Helping to maintain a building or providing a service to help those that need the word, is an important investment. Freely giving the word of the Lord is what is needed today. Still many ask what is in it for me?

This question is answered in the Bible. If your doing it to get to heaven forget it and if you're doing it because you love the word of God, go for it. Building treasures in heaven is a popular term for not being compensated for the work you are doing here on earth, but rewarded in heaven. Being a servant of the Lord requires you to volunteer your services and give freely of your money to help all people.

Jesus makes this clear in the above verse. Still many try to profit from the less fortunate, the least, as Jesus would say. Jesus tells that the first will be last and the last first. Many do not understand that still pertains to our society today. They guide their lives with the goal of great wealth and fame. Sadly many of these people claim to be good Christians.

Are you giving to help those that don't know the Lord. Does your financial plan have spreading the word of God as it's goal.

Lord, help me be a person that cares about the least in our society. Help me give the word of God to all that will hear.

*A*nd we know that all things work together for the good to those who love God, to those who are called according to His purpose. *Romans 8:28 NKJV*

Believe while others doubt. Persist while others are quitting. William Arthur Ward used these words when he wrote the Winners Handbook. As Christians we are already winners. Your circle of friends and how you interact as a Christian is what forms the effect you have on your community. How you interact with friends, family and your church guide your life, making your life what it is today. I can only hope you are reaching out to those that don't know the Lord. This activity is as important as the study of the Bible.

Growing as a Christian is what we all strive for in our lives. Still we see people that have found a comfort level that causes them not to take risks and grow, they do not reach out to those that do not know the Lord. This comfort level can be brought on by your circle of friends or the malaise that has come over your church. Malaise is defined as a condition of general weakness or discomfort, often marking the onset of disease.

This condition, this malaise, causes inaction and can become a mind set. People may feel that problems are out of the reach of the body of the church. Believing we can make a positive change in our community and in the lives of others through the word of God is number one. Believe while others doubt, persist while others are quitting is what we have to *do to facilitate change. Why? Because we're already winners, we are Christians.*

Lord, help me rekindle the fire that has burned so bright, so the light from that fire will reach all who are lost.

*B*ut whoever drinks of the water that I shall give him will never thirst. But the water that I shall give him will become in him a fountain of water springing up into everlasting life. John 4:14 NKJV

How many times do we go to the well before we drink from the life giving water. We seek change and may know of Jesus, we may even believe in a God. But our irresponsible behavior and our quest for pleasure along with man's weak minded sinful nature cause us to be separated from God. But He is the source of all life giving water, the water of change. People become enslaved to pleasure and dishonesty. They seek peace and the tranquility that can only be provided by God. Through faith in Jesus you can receive the life giving water that brings about change and provides tranquility.

Many thirst for this water but do not drink when it is offered. Personal pleasure and man's sinful nature insulate him from real change. Like a cocoon our rebellious and sinful nature forms a impenetrable layer that keeps us from a personal relationship with God. Through our faith in God and quiet time in prayer a metamorphosis will take place. Like a caterpillar becomes a butterfly we can be more like Jesus. Our minds will slowly transform into ones of knowledge and wisdom. Our hearts will be filled with kindness and compassion for our fellow man. We will lay down all the pleasures of man. With a clear mind and a changed heart, we will thank God for His life giving water and our new found changed life.

Have you promised to change and fallen short over and over again? Is the problem you, or are you blaming someone else? God wants the best for his creations, just drink His life giving water.

Lord, help me change my sinful ways and lay down my pursuit of the pleasures of man. Please give me life changing water

S o then, my beloved brethren let every man be swift to hear, and slow to speak, slow to wrath; for the wrath of man does not produce the righteousness of God. James 1-19 NKJV

Most people don't listen and when you give advice it falls on deaf ears. I try to be a better listener and many times write a story about something someone has told me. Talking to the man that owns the guitar shop is a great source of information and inspiration for my writing. He told me of a young man that had been bullied at school. One day he got his books knocked out of his hand by a bully, a young man came over and helped him pick up his books. They started talking and over the next few days they became friends.

Time passed and the two young men were graduating from high school. The young man who had been bullied was now the valedictorian of his class. During his speech he told the audience that he owed his success to his friend for helping him pick up those books that day and for his kindness and friendship that followed. He said that he owed everything to this young man because on that day he was so depressed that he had planned to go home and kill himself.

Jesus tells us to love thy brother as thyself. Many don't do this and many shy away from any meaningful interaction with those outside their group of friends. Today it is more important than ever to reach out to others with the kind and caring word of the Lord. As you heard in this story your friendship may be saving a life of someone who didn't receive the love of his fellow man.

Whether you were a bully or were bullied God want's to show you his love. Start reading the Bible and ask God into your heart.

Lord, put people in my path that need your love and guidance I will tell them that with you all things are possible.

*B*ut whoever has this world's goods, and sees his brother in need, and shuts up his heart from him, how does the love of God abide in him? My little children, let us not love in word and tongue, but in deed and truth, 1 John 3:17-18 NKJV

There are many that reach out to help, but many don't hear of their good deeds. Everywhere you go today there are people that could use a kind word. They could use a hand up not a hand out. They could use the message of the risen Lord Jesus Christ. At our church the message has been made clear and many reach out to lead and guide those that don't know the Lord. Many provide assistance to those in financial need.

One day I was talking with a man at church telling him how a young women needed some financial assistance and a uplifting Christian message. That week he went to her job and talked to her. He left her some bread and pastries that he delivers. This is the type of things Christians do, they reach out to help others. Today many are in need financially and spiritually. People so often don't feel they have someone who cares about them. Caring Christians can solve this problem by providing a message of love and kindness that is Jesus Christ.

Reaching out is what we all must do as believing Christians. Jesus came to save mankind and because he did I would think we would want to be generous, caring and kind. Today more and more people need assistance. Many young people feel there is no hope of a good job or the ability to get a college education. As like minded Christians it is *our duty to reach out to those less fortunate. We can start by giving the word of God to those that don't know it.*

Lord, thank you for the man who cares to help those in need.

*T*his is what the Lord says, "He who appoints the sun to shine by day, decrees the moon and stars to shine by night, stirs up the sea so that its waves roar-the Lord Almighty is His name.*

The future world envisioned in the past is what I often remember. We were required to read 1984 when I was in school. Science fiction and the space program fueled the imaginations of many a young person. Today with all our advances the vision of the future from the past has not been realized. We haven't colonized the moon. Mars exploration is a far way off along with thousands of futuristic ideas from flying cars to anti gravity boots.

While watching movies with my grandsons I realized that so many of the movie ideas are just improved visions of the pasts vision of the future. Many aren't that good; there seems to be more explosions and more destruction in our current vision of the future. More flames and more shooting small caliber bullets at large targets. A future that is computer controlled with large amounts of people viewing screens. Where foot soldiers have little success against their foes no matter how high tech their weaponry. Mainly some superior force in the form of a super hero is needed to win the battle and save the city or world.

Sadly in the augmented reality of our computer generated, super hero obsessed, society we have become blind to the great creation of God. The beauty of nature and the grandeur of the landscape of this planet. Many stare at their handheld device to check the weather as the raindrops soak their clothes, without ever looking at the sky. God is the real superhero!

What is in store for man in the future? You are an integral part of how it will play out. Remember God is the creator of all things and how you manage the world he has entrusted you with is all important.

Lord, help me make the future better for everyone.

"*Because he loves me," Says the Lord "I will rescue him; I will protect him, for he acknowledges My name. He will call upon me, and I will answer him. I will be with him in trouble. I will deliver him and honor him. With long life will I satisfy him and show him my salvation. Psalm 91 14-16 NIV*

Some people don't see the good their doing. They lead by example, their kind and caring, but still they feel that all they do doesn't change lives. I like saying so many go out to change lives but few go out to change themselves. God can only change others; you can only change yourself with the word of God.

So often we are doing far more than we imagine. Our actions and words set a standard that is an example to many. Our humble and kind demeanor shows others the path to travel toward a spirit filled life. God puts people in our path, guiding us to be a better person. He also uses those people as a way for us to strengthen our faith and gain wisdom. Your self confidence and wisdom is what guides people to change through the word of God.

If you feel your actions aren't working or all your efforts are in vain, God may have other plans. He may be teaching you perseverance or self-confidence. The toughest battles are with our own self doubts. With God in our hearts we can meet all challenges head-on, even the ones of self-confidence. You may feel like you have failed, but God is just training you to be a team player.

Are you working toward change today as a member of God's team? Are you gaining confidence and wisdom along the way?

Lord, help me share a message of change through knowledge in your word and strength from your spirit.

For what man knows the things of man except the spirit of the man which is in him? Even so no one knows the things of God except the spirit of God. Now we have received, not the spirit of the world, but the spirit that is from God, that we might know the things that have been freely given to us by God. 1 Corinthians 2 11-12 NKJV

The first snowfall of the year is often a thing of beauty. Trees coated with a thick layer of snow bend low under the weight. Moist flakes strike your face and cling to your eyelashes. All the leaves that graced the ground are covered with a blanket of white. There is a stillness in the air that only comes with wet new snow.

Many messages about the beauty of nature are preached to show the majesty of God. Snow seems to be the best example of change for my writings. I often walk the snowy streets and paths in my area enjoying the beauty of a new snowfall. I gaze out over fields and woodlands enjoying the bright majestic landscape.

Sadly for many winter's beauty is a sign of dread, hardship and financial burden. For some though the snow brings beauty to the landscape and financial gain to their business. Being ready for winter is a metaphor for how God wants you to run your life. To be ready for change and have a spirit of thankfulness for that change. Like the verse above God gives you the spirit to see how he views the world, but we know many today that still view it through man's eyes.

In this season of giving are you giving the encouraging word of Jesus Christ to those you meet along the way? As the *song says, Oh! Precious is the flow that makes me white as snow nothing but the blood of Jesus. Are you telling people how they can change their life through Christ?*

Lord, help me make my thoughts as white and pure as the new fallen snow.

"*But let each one examine his own work, and then he will have rejoicing in himself alone, and not in another. For each one shall bear his own load." Galatians 6:4-5*

The young pastor told me, "People that stop by the church seem to be able to have their problems solved with ten dollars." I told him we call that S.C.M. stray cat mentality. Like a stray cat looks for food people look for easy money and many times it's from the people that can least afford to be giving. Some become a nuisance and make you feel like your the only person that can improve their life.

Their life can only be improved when they take control of it. Personal responsibility for your own life is what God commands. We get asked for money and sometimes we do give out money but we always give a strong message based in the word of God. Sadly many today are focused on the pleasures of man and want someone else to pay for their bad behavior.

People on fixed incomes and those who are underemployed can be in need of financial help. Having to fall back on outreach programs for food assistance and help with living expenses. Many of these people would choose a source of income before they would choose charity. Drive, ambition and concern motivate many elderly and low income people to reach out to those in need. This act of kindness helps both parties.

A handout is not always helpful when it comes to getting people on track with personal finances. There is no substitute for a steady income. Being able to count on a fixed amount of income from a steady job can build confidence and give structure to a once unstructured life. The word of God is the foundation of an improved life and work provides the building material of change.

Lord, help us find the answer to the tough question of how to help those who do not know how to help themselves.

*T*wenty nine years ago with the Holy Spirit as my guide. I entered at the portico of Genesis and walked down the corridor of the Old Testament art galleries, where pictures of Noah, Abraham, Moses, Joseph, Isaac, Jacob and Daniel are hanging on the wall. I passed into the music room of the Psalms where the sweet spirit sweeps the keyboard of nature. Until every reed and pipe in God's great organ respond to the harp of David the sweet singer in Israel. I entered into the chamber of Ecclesiastes where the voice of the preacher is heard. I entered the conservatory of Sharon the lily of the valley. Sweet spices filled and perfumed my life. I entered the business office of Proverbs and on into the observatory of the prophets were I saw telescopes of various sizes pointing to far off events. Concentrating on the bright and morning star which was to arise above the moonlight hills of Judea for our salvation and redemption. I entered the audience room of the King of Kings. Catching a vision written by Matthew, Mark, Luke and John. I stepped into the correspondence room where Paul, Peter, James and John were writing their epistles. I stepped into the throne room of revelation where tower the glittering peaks. Where sits the King of Kings upon the throne of glory with the healing of the nations in his hand. And I cried out, "All hail the power of Jesus' name. Let angels prostrate fall. Bring forth the royal diadem and crown Him Lord of all." Billy Sunday Baseball player and famous preacher.

That is the Bible in a nutshell. Billy Sunday couldn't have said it any better. This verse is one of the most beautiful *descriptions of our walk with God. Years of study and understanding went into this page. Some may find that wisdom and understanding gives them all that they can ask for in this world. Studying the Bible and prayer will help you in your journey to draw closer to God.*

Lord, in my walk with Jesus help me find the simple truth.

*S*o when He saw them, He said "Go, show yourselves to the priests. And so it was that as they went they were cleansed. And one of them, when he saw that he was healed, returned, and with a loud voice glorified God, and fell on his face at His feet, giving Him thanks. And he was a Samaritan. Luke 17:14-16 NKJV*

In God's great plan we are set on a path with people that will change your life. My life has greatly changed since I first came to know the Lord. Difficult decisions, concerns about others and faith in God improves our lives. That faith gives us the strength, honesty and love that we learn in our walk with Jesus. When we find someone special that helps and guides us on our path we can't help being thankful.

A young woman stood up at the funeral for our pastor who had died quite suddenly and told how he took time to help her understand what God wanted for her life and how faith in God could make that all happen. She had just been baptized a few weeks before and was one of the last people he baptized. Our pastors life was one of service to the church and he lived his life so she could be baptized. That is what Jesus talks about, to be a servant, to live your life to help others. How many were helped and how many thanked God for that blessing can't be counted by man.

God put you on a path for a reason, many would say it is to be changed, others say to be healed. I would say it is to meet people that have true Christian love and to give thanks for finding those people.

Lord, help me to be a better servant, giving thanks and guiding others to your love.

*G*od has not given me a spirit of fear, but of power, love, and a sound mind. 2 Timothy 1:7 KJV

I haven't stood in your shoes but I have felt your pain. When I saw the pastor kneeling in prayer at the altar I could tell that he was overcome with sadness. Problems at home and work along with a very ill mother had almost become to much for him to handle.

Many of us have been overwhelmed by sadness and depression brought on by a host of problems. I usually start my conversation by telling people I don't know what is in their heart but I can tell it is broken. I have that feeling quite frequently as problems and grief sometimes overcome me. Seeing a very ill friend in the hospital or hearing a story about the loss of a loved one can start my mind racing.

My mind is racing, but if I use my mind I can win the race. Sadness and depression can lead you on a journey where your thoughts rehash everything that emotionally affected your life. You can't change the past has always been my message. The past is a dead end street where problems can't be solved. Living in the present and working toward change is the path to a better life. God's word will guide you towards real and lasting change. God wants you to draw closer to Him even though our natural desire is to have Him draw closer to us.

Are you drawing closer to God today? Are you reaching out to people that are in need of the word of God?

Lord, help me to not live in the past. Still my racing mind; make my path straight and my way clear.

The journey of a thousands miles starts with a single step. That is a phrase we have used since I first read Dr. Richard Carlson's book, Don't Worry. Make Money. The message of his books are to help you make a difference in your life and this book has made a difference in my life. I have given this book to many people that want a changed life, but they never take time to read it's helpful stories. I have even gone to the extent of memorizing sayings from it to use when trying to motivate people to change.

You can't always motivate people to change even though many search for a better life. People must search for change to find a better life. In a quest for money and fame many have found it takes a lot of hard work. Gaining knowledge and wisdom people find it takes time and money. Building a reputation requires honesty and dedication. People that work their entire lives to have the life they can be proud of find that they have fallen short time and time again. Many find that they had to fail before they understood what success really was.

Reading a motivational book is a great start and gives an incentive to make changes in your life. Most people don't follow through and end up just in a different rutt on the road to change. Real change is in the word of God. The Creator's motivational book for those with unfulfilled lives. True success can only be had through prayer and following the law of God, it says so in the Bible. Many want real change but never take time to study the book that has all the answers, that book is the Bible.

If you're going to take that single step toward change have your Bible in your hand. That is the only way you'll have true success.

Lord, let me step out for change and travel thousands of miles telling others about the word of God.

*F*ear not, that you be not judged. For with what judgment you judge, you will be judged; and with the measure you use, it will be measured back to you. Matthew 7:1-2 NKJV

Turmoil sometimes overtakes your life. It's the snowball effect like you see in the cartoons. The snowball gets bigger and bigger then it rolls over you. In the cartoon you stick to the snowball as it gets bigger and rolls faster down the hill to disaster. Life sometimes has moments that are similar to this illustration.

Many times people in your life influence this turmoil. The real problem is you let them. They make you feel obligated to do things you wouldn't normally do. People present an argument that you are somehow responsible for their problems. How we deal with these people can be difficult and stressful. Often it is the I know I am not doing what I should or just help me one more time type of reasoning. Most of the time it's you've got money and I don't argument. Many people lack responsibility for their own actions. Some like to use the blame game as a way to make you feel guilty. This form of manipulation is bad for both parties involved.

Most people's problems can be solved with ten dollars or so you would think, but in the long run their problems will only get worse. To change we must live in the present and tell others to take charge of their lives and finances. Drug use is a big factor in the people we interact with. Lack of personal responsibility is the other problem. The idea that they should get something for nothing or you should fund *their irresponsible lifestyle seems to be a root cause of many problems.*

You can learn from the past but the present is where the work is done. Working toward change is what makes for a better life. Seeking God is what is truly the beginning of real change. Encourage those that ask for assistance, to seek the word of God.

*T*hese things that I have spoken to you, That in Me you may have peace. In the world you will have tribulation; but be of good cheer, I have overcome the world. John 16:33 NKJV

The problem with everyday troubles that befall most people is that they are not prepared or equipped to deal with them. Financial problems, medical problems and work related issues can turn our lives upside down. Having a solid faith in God can be all that is required to help turn your life around.

Asking God about purchasing big ticket items can reduce financial woes. When illness befalls a family, prayer and faith can reduce stress and improve the outcome of the most difficult medical problem. Dealing with problems at work can be tempered with the word of God. Love thy neighbor as thyself is always number one in any discussion. Combine that with forgiveness and you have an unbeatable combination. Use this plan and work should go pretty smooth.

Let God be part of your everyday life and you will find the problems will fade away. Prayer and study will help you make your daily life into what you have always wanted. A family that is guided by the word of God will have fewer problems than those that go it alone. Your life is like a ship on the ocean and the word of God is like a compass. If you do not have a compass, you end up lost. Learn what God wants for you today and start studying His word. It will become the compass you will use to guide your life.

Are you prepared to deal with problems that may arise in your family's life? Are you drawing closer to God using His word as a compass for your life?

Lord, if I stray off course, please guide me safely back to Your word.

*T*his poor man cried out, and the Lord heard him, And saved him out of his troubles. Psalm 34:6 NKJV

Plagued by the past, many people as they get older reflect on all the negatives that seem to have shaped their life. For many people childhood troubles such as abusive parents, lack of money and early work experiences seem to be the negative experiences most people talk about. Many had parents that were abusive and neglectful. Those growing up in homes where alcohol and drugs fueled the problems are also quite common.

Most of the people we talk to had difficult childhoods. Almost all of them have made a good life for themselves. Still the memories of their childhood weigh heavy on their hearts. Regrets, unresolved anger and grief can be a millstone around their neck. God has a time line in the Bible and it only moves forward. God doesn't go back and change the past. But for many revisiting the past is an everyday occurrence. For some people thoughts of lost love, memories of sadness and sorrow consume many hours everyday. There is a clear message in the Bible, that is to live in the present and plan for a better tomorrow.

Are you focused on today and planning for tomorrow? When the Lord is there to guide you there is no reason to look back on the past as the cause of all your troubles. Are you trusting God with all your heart?

I will praise You, O Lord, with my whole heart; I will tell of all Your marvelous works. I will be glad and rejoice in

You: I will sing praise to Your name, O Most High. Psalm 9:1-2 NKJV

Lord, Help me to calm the minds of those who live in the troubles of the past with Your soothing words.

*T*herefore if any man be in Christ, he is a new creature; old things have passed away; all things have become new. 2 Corinthians 5:17 NKJV

Wanting the best for your children involves wanting the best for yourself. Many young people face problems that we have dealt with and some that we have not overcome. Drugs and alcohol are the most common along with personal responsibility. The problem of fidelity in a relationship can also be a stumbling block for many. When giving advice to young people we need to examine our own lives.

Helping someone to change is a difficult task. Honesty is the most important part of facilitating that change. We often find when talking to others that a part of our life could use improvement. When it comes to drugs and alcohol I can only advise a zero tolerance. I have never met a person who's life was improved by the use of drugs or alcohol. As many reach out to help their children they find out that some areas in their own life could use improvement. Many have avoided these personal shortcomings that have caused problems throughout their lives.

Marital relations, personal honesty and finances are common issues that come to light when reaching out to troubled young adults or your own children. Personal honesty and personal responsibility issues can also come to light in your life as you reach out to help a troubled young adult. The beginning of change starts with God. His word is the compass that will help us find our way back to a truly meaningful life. If your reaching out to help someone today expressing *love and compassion, you're already on that path of change. Reaching out to help others is the beginning of improving your own life.*

Lord, help me overcome my shortcomings and change my life with Your word. Help me be honest, loving and kind to all.

B *ut Jesus looked at them and said, "With men it is impossible, But not with God; for with God all things are possible." Mark 10:27 NKJV*

The rich young man ran to Jesus and asked how he could receive eternal life. To him that may have seemed like something that could be easily given by a great man like Jesus. He may have thought that with eternal life he could enjoy all the wealth and power he had accumulated over the years. Jesus answered and told him the truth about what eternal happiness is all about. It is not about money, power or fame. It is about a close personal relationship with God.

Jesus tells him if he wants eternal life he has to put down those things of man and follow His example reaching out to all that are in need of the word of God. Why did he tell him this, because he loved him. The young man had tried to do all that was right, but had fallen into the trap of money, power and fame. The difference was he wanted to have eternal life. This can only be achieved through faith in God not the works of man. Those works are wealth, power and fame which can easily control you.

Jesus tells him that he has to take up the cross and follow him. To live his life in the pursuit of truth and justice even if it leads to death. The cross had already become a symbol of this before Jesus' death. The young man is not content with having to give up his riches and possibly his life for the eternal life that Jesus offers. Jesus then uses this man's reaction as an example to His disciples. Telling them that it is easier for a camel to pass through the eye of a needle than for a rich man to enter Heaven. To which they answered, "Who then can be saved?" The message is clear, you can be saved all you have to do is lay down the things of man and follow Jesus.

Lord, help me to pick up my cross and follow You.

*L*et us examine our ways, and turn back to the Lord; Let us lift up our hearts and hands to God in Heaven. Lam. 3:40-41 NKJV

Each year we see a celebration that is called fat Tuesday or Mardi Gras. This celebration of bad behavior, lust and excess is where the hedonist would find solace. People like to associate with those who have similar interests and this event has grown.

I met a young man that said he was a hedonist. Before he found God. His life had been centered around the pursuit of pleasure. Drugs, alcohol and promiscuous sex was all his life was focused on. Serious trouble is lurking in this lifestyle and many can't break free from this quest for pleasure.

A friend of mine says Hedonists worship at the altar of bad behavior. God plays no part in these peoples lives but he never abandons them. His increasing love and desire for their change causes many to see the error of their ways. Tired and weary, broken and confused the revelers at the all-night pursuit of pleasure ask God to save them from themselves.

With exalted pride on a float they ride as dancers spin and sway. Two worlds collide with shame laid aside, as man's lust and pride are celebrated through the day. In hearts that hear no wrong, the music swells as the desire of men turns into song. Hell bent on pleasure, revelers throw their pearls before the swine. And then one day with great dismay when pleasure can't be found. The silence screams as dreams die slowly on the vine. Upon this ground their friends not found, all run from the failure of their quest. Their thoughts *so foul have come to ruin as metal turned to rust. The fading sound of deceitful dreams are overcome with deep regret. With fortunes spent on this lustful quest the reveling crowd in their regret are trampled into dust. G.P.T.*

*T*hen he cried and said, Father Abraham, have mercy on me, and send Lazarus that he may dip the tip of his finger in water and cool my tongue; for I am tormented in this flame. But Abraham said, Son, remember that in your lifetime you received your good things, and likewise Lazarus evil things; but now he is comforted and you are tormented. And besides all this, between us and you is a great gulf fixed, so those that who want to pass from here to you cannot, nor can those from there pass to us. Luke 16:24-26 NKJV

Hell has driven out the wonder that most would call love; it cannot be restored by the descending of a dove. For the inequities of evil reign in their hearts supreme forever separated by a chasm the Lord hears not their screams. G.P.T.

We point to heaven singing it's all about Him while we think how is this benefiting me. We give a dollar to the poor and feel we are doing our part. Asked about a verse we say you can look at it in different ways because we haven't taken time to understand what it says. Looking to the Lord for answers that we already know in our heart because we don't address the problem with sincere prayer. Worshiping God and applying his word does not play a part in our business and in our home but at church it's all about Him.

We all fall short that is a fact; it is written in the Bible. Through prayer and worship it can be all about Him. Our home and business should be a place where the word of God is all important. Ask God to give you a renewed outlook before a gulf or chasm is fixed between you and God.

Have you asked God to make it all about Him in your Life?

Lord, help me be faithful and sincere because it is all about You.

*W*ork with your own hands as we commanded you...
*that you may lack nothing. 1 Thessalonians 4:11-12
NKJV*

Like a car sitting by the side of the road out of gas many people are in need of a fill up. God's word is like the gas you need to run your car so you can continue on your journey. God's word can provide a fill up of high octane motivation to propel you to the destination of your dreams. To launch out on your own to see what you can do, not what you can have people do for you. Ask not what people can do for you ask what you can do for people is a good saying to keep in mind as you head down the highway of life.

For those who feel like that car, broke down at the at the side of the road an inspirational message of encouragement may be all they need. People that have had to pull off the road for a health condition, personal problem and financial reasons all need our help and encouragement. The message should be one that focuses on God and prayer. But that message must be based on a personal relationship with the risen Lord Jesus Christ and promote self confidence. This will build personal responsibility and a new found ambition for meaningful change.

The journey of a thousand miles begins with a single step. Sadly many need to call for roadside assistance to get them back on the highway of life. We as like minded Christians must reach out to those that have had to pull off the highway of life. With the word of God, your love and caring hopefully will have them back on the road in no time.

Are you going out on a service call today to give the word of God to someone in need? Are your working on your message of encouragement to help and guide some poor lost soul, that maybe only you can help?

Lord, give me the wisdom that is needed to solve these difficult problems we face today.

A nd we know that all things work together for the good to those that love God, to those who are called to His purpose. Romans 8:28 NKJV

Over the last year we have been promoting direct giving. That is a long standing idea of you giving directly to someone in need. You can still give all you want to groups and organizations so they can help others. But your personal gift of money or help along with a Christian message can help bring you closer to God.

People do this quite frequently and promote this idea in those that they helped. The recipients of this help sometimes call it pay it forward after a popular movie. But what we encourage is to give a strong Christian message along with your gift of money or service. Many don't know the Lord even though they express a belief in God. There are groups focused on the homeless and those that need food, but still more is needed. Education, wisdom and generosity can bring forth real change that will benefit all that have a need. The word of God is the most important message.

A man stops by a lawn mower shop and gives a young girl at the cash register food and a Christian message. This action helps her in providing for her five children. Two men at a guitar shop give a message of perseverance and provide encouragement to all that come in. They give a lesson that through work you can achieve your dreams. The owner of a small restaurant gives food and clothes to those out on the street and his steady customers join in. This is what direct *giving is all about looking at everyone as a person that you could help and to look at them as a friend.*

Are you making new friends on your Christian walk with Jesus? Are you seeking out people that could benefit from your generosity?

Lord, help us make the right choices, those that will do the most good.

*A*nd when Jesus came to the place, He looked up and saw him, and said to him, "Zacchaeus, make haste and come down, for today I must stay at your house." Luke 19:5 NKJV

I guess you never know when Jesus is coming to your house. Zacchaeus the tax collector was a well known man maybe not for the right reasons, but he was a Jew just like Jesus, a son of Abraham. Why did Jesus seek out Zacchaeus? Because he was lost. Today many men wait for the kingdom of God, but are what we would call lost. They believe in God but do not fully understand. Many seek but do not find. God is the creator of all and the Bible is his instruction manual. Our personal relationship with God is what the Kingdom of Heaven is all about. It is the life changing power.

Just like Jesus picked a rich tax collector who was short of stature he could have picked anyone that truly believes. To be picked you have to know in your heart what your doing is wrong and you have to want God to change you. Today many seek but do not find the life changing power. Many times it's because a confusing message of beliefs and doctrine is being given by a group or organization. The real change only comes with belief in the risen Lord Jesus Christ. Often a rich man knows he's wrong but so often a poor man feels he is being wronged.

Many of us seek change but don't realize that it is in our grasp. Through prayer and our faith in the risen Lord even the most dishonest person can change. Ask God through prayer to change you, taking the burden from your shoulders.

If you have chosen him as your Savior ask Him to choose you. God knows what is in your heart. Choose a quiet place where you are alone and through prayer ask him to save you from your sinful wicked self.

Have you wronged your friends and family? Are you ashamed at all the things you are now doing?

Lord, I know you are seeking me out. Come and stay at my house as an honored guest.

What is dishonesty? In business it is intentionally concealing something from stockholders, partners or creditors. On a financial report it is the lack of full disclosure. That is not telling the whole story whether it is good or bad. The sad part is there isn't anything good about dishonesty. Lives are affected by people that are motivated by greed and power. Sadly dishonesty has moved into areas that should be bastions of honesty. As people strive for success the want of money and power seem to be at the forefront of this problem. Well intentioned people can easily veer off the path into deceit and dishonesty.

Many religious organizations, public assistance programs and not for profit medical groups find themselves under more and more scrutiny every day. What starts many of these problems is the tremendous amount of money that can be generated by people giving. God loves a cheerful giver, but he hates those that steal from the poor. In America servicing the poor and needy for some can be a profitable business. Beyond the basic idea of helping poor and disadvantaged people the not for profit neighborhood develop groups are making real inroads in social change.

Like all businesses safeguards need to be put in place to monitor the not for profit organizations finances, both in house and independently. A good accountant is needed along with a independent auditor. Misuse of funds, waste and misappropriation can slowly creep into an organization that is based on well intentioned giving. Supporting political candidates, social activism and lobbying for the change of laws can all be areas where festering dishonesty can run rampant.

Safeguard yourself from dishonesty creeping into your organization. As the sums of money collected become larger and larger, waste and misappropriation can rapidly increase. If your planning to start a new service or outreach organization remember to be a good steward of the money going to the poor.

A generous man will himself be blessed, for he shares his food with the poor. Proverbs 22:9 NIV

The other day we heard our pastor talk about being one family of God. As Christians we are one cohesive group of like minded individuals. What happens to many groups of Christians is a mind set of bitterness and unforgiving overcomes them. Problems of personal preference and direction of leadership can drive a wedge between church members.

We are blessed because we can provide the food of life, the word of the risen Lord Jesus Christ. For many Christians forgiving others for the wrongs they have done is a difficult task. Jesus tells Peter that forgiving is all important because God forgives those that have sinned. Bitterness and resentment can lead the way in conversations with someone who feels they have been wronged. Peter wronged Jesus by lying to him and then not admitting he even knew him. Jesus knew that Peter would fail because man is a failed creature. Jesus forgave him and blessed him with the great ability to preach and do miracles.

Christians all need to work together as one group, putting aside differences that have caused a divide in their beliefs. A great gulf or chasm has grown between believers in many churches. How we bridge this divide is how we understand the message of God.

Are you working toward understanding while reaching out to your Christian brothers? Have you forgiven those that have wronged you?

Lord help me show forgiveness striving toward love and kindness toward my fellow man.

*N*ow he could do no mighty work there, except that he laid his hands on a few sick people and healed them. And He marveled because of their unbelief. Mark 6:5-6 NKJV

I marvel everyday at peoples unbelief as I'm sure you do. Jesus goes to his hometown and finds himself not well received. A prophet has no honor in his own town. They didn't believe in the power of Jesus.

Unbelief is what keeps us from entering Heaven. To draw people into a discussion about God at a street fair a church had a riddle printed on a banner. What do rocks eat? What do dead people dream? What can you do enough of to get to heaven? The answer I was told was nothing. This was a message about works or deeds. Nothing was described by Aristotle as what rocks dream. So I get that idea but to get to Heaven you have to believe. You have to believe that God created you and created Heaven. You have to believe in his Son, who died for you so you could go to Heaven.

Telling people that there is nothing you can do to go to Heaven sets people on the wrong path. Jesus as stated above did not find honor in his hometown, they did not believe and in turn people did not receive favor in the form of blessings and miracles. What you have to do is believe with all your heart that Jesus is Lord. When it comes to going to Heaven doing nothing would be described as disbelief in God, Jesus and the Holy Spirit. What can you do to get to Heaven ask God to come into your heart.

Are you giving a clear message today? Are you encouraging people to come to know the Lord?

Lord, help me help others to come to know Your love, so they can have the hope that is eternal life in Heaven.

Your iniquities have separated you from God; and your sins have hidden His face from you. Isaiah 59:2 NKJV

So often we hear people complain about financial problems that have thrown their world upside down. But where is God in these peoples lives is the first question that should be asked. Many claim to know the Lord but they find solace in the accumulation of things. Many say they find pleasure in God's words and seek pleasure from alcohol or food. Still others say they delight in the word but find themselves delighting in promiscuous sex and the use of drugs. When you put down these vices is when you start to know God.

God needs to be number one in your life and in the lives of your family members. Many today don't fully commit to God because they want the pleasures of man. Sex, food, drugs and alcohol all have power over man. When the spirit of God is truly in your heart, it is easy to turn away from the pleasures of man. Ask God to come into your heart to remove the desire for these things.

Seek a personal relationship with God ask him through prayer to come into your heart and free you from the things of man. Problems with money ask God. Problems with fidelity ask God. Problems with drugs or alcohol ask God. Prayer is the answer and the power of the Holy Spirit is the cure.

Are you serving two masters, God and the pleasures of man? Have you sincerely asked God to remove these things from your life? Are your prayers, prayers for change?

Lord help me love you and not the pleasures of man. Guide me to live a life free from the things of man.

When God's people are in need, be ready to help them. Always be eager to practice hospitality. Romans 12:13 NLT

Life is a compromise, an area where black and white do not exist. It is an area where there are just shades of gray. God the creator of all has a plan for us, but how we reach our goal is achieved through a lot of trial and error. We are all works in progress and as we get older many of the things we held true have faded away. Complex ideas may now seem simple and simple problems seem more complex.

Many times our problems are made worse by bitterness and lack of forgiveness. In this rapidly changing world where God's word is not always practiced, turmoil can overwhelm our life. The black and white word of God is the anchor we need in our decision making process. Forgiveness and the kindness of like-minded Christians is not a compromise. It is what God commands us to do, it is the work we were created for.

Today God's people are in need. They're in need of all believers in Christ acting as a unified group, showing love and kindness to all. Forgiving those that have wronged them and helping those that can't help themselves. As Christians we must work toward the betterment of all mankind, not just the people we like.

Have you reached out to someone who does not know the Lord? Have you shown forgiveness to someone who has wronged you?

Lord help me to continue to love my fellow man and show forgiveness and love to all.

*M*y wife often wonders why I mow the lawns at two different churches. I tell her it gives me an opportunity to talk to people that need assistance and don't know the Lord. I have a strange sense of humor and try out different ideas of help and guidance. Our message is one of honesty and personal responsibility. Sadly many of the people that stop to talk to me just want money.

A man was walking by one day and stopped to ask me if I could help him out. He needed some money so he could sleep at a friends house. I jokingly told him that I had spent all my money on lotto tickets, cigarettes, drugs and alcohol. I told him that I only get ten dollars for mowing the lawn. And that I felt compelled to give that money back in the church collection today. "Why?" he asked. I told him it was because God had forgiven me for foolishly wasting my money on lotto, cigarettes, drugs and alcohol.

"Man you must be crazy your mowing all this for ten bucks and then giving that money back to the church." he said in disgust. "Why would you do such a dumb thing and waste that money?" he said. I told him a lot of people spend all their money on lotto, cigarettes, drugs and alcohol. "No," he said, "giving back that ten dollars to the church, I could of used that."

I would say I'm blessed having an opportunity to tell people about how God can change their lives. That the pleasures of man can't satisfy like the word of God. And that God will forgive you if you sincerely ask him to. The first thing you have to understand is many people that come to a church for help don't understand that God can help them; their just looking for money or food.

Are you reaching out to help the needy in your area? Are you giving a message of honesty and personal responsibility along with the word of God?

Lord, give me patience to help those that don't know that the word of God can solve all problems.

"*Have I not commanded you? Be strong and of good courage; do not be afraid, nor dismayed, for the Lord your God is with you wherever you go.*" *Joshua 1:9 NKJV*

God is right there with you guiding you to make the right decisions. For some those decisions are focused only on success in the things of man. Money, power and status lead the way as the banner we call success. We hold up our house and possessions as a sign of self worth. Education and job title as signs of status. Without a foundation in the word of God these things are meaningless. God has commanded you to be strong and of good courage because He is with you.

God wants you to think more about Him than you do about your house or car. He wants you to think more about Him than food and drink. Sadly in today's world people are viewed as just consumers and in many cases they have become consumed by the things of man.. A nice house and car are good things that people work toward. Good food and drink are a reward for all your hard work. Sadly this is where the trouble begins. The fact is many today fall into the trap of consumption where material things and pleasure are more important than God.

Success and faith in God go hand in hand. Are you reaching out to God so he can guide you to success? Are you being consumed by the pleasures of man?

Lord, give me the strength to follow you and too not fall prey to the excesses of mankind.

*F*or if they do these things in the green wood, what will be done in the dry. Luke 23:31 NKJV

Many of the words of Luke seem strange or different, but we forget that Luke was not a Jew he was a gentile writer that wanted to give an accurate account of Jesus and Paul. Some people feel he wrote his gospel to help free Paul from persecution and jail in Rome.

Luke had never met Jesus but through his research and interviews he was able to make a complete story that is far more descriptive than those of Matthew and Mark. Luke has a richer and more powerful view of the effects that the words of Jesus had on mankind. His other great contribution is The Book of Acts which describes the formation of early Christianity.

The verse above is the language of a carpenter. The verse is a warning to the Daughters of Jerusalem. Much like Paul's letters these writings give a clear message that applies to the times they were written. The great thing is they're as current in their subject matter today as they were nearly two thousand years ago.

Luke was interested in how the belief in Jesus spread from a Jewish sect to a gentile religion. Luke even tells us where the people were first called Christians which was in his hometown. Having traveled with Paul he saw first hand what was taking place in the descriptions of the letters to the early churches. Luke gives us a treasure trove of information written to convince one man about Jesus and Paul's ministry.

Take time to study Luke's writings. Compare them to the other Gospels you won't be disappointed.

Lord, give me the power to understand and the energy to teach what I have learned.

*F*or I know the plans I have for you, declares the Lord, plans for welfare not for evil, to give you a future and a hope. Jeremiah 29:11 ESV

Growing up in a small town when I was young we didn't get to do many of the things that people now take for granted. My mother would entertain us with stories of her childhood. She would also tell about all the movies she saw and all the big bands she'd seen in her youth. As an entertainment critic for her school paper she had fallen in love with movies. Clark Gable and Errol Flynn were two of her favorite actors and she had seen some of their movies as many as ten times.

When she grew up you had to use your imagination. Radio was the driving force in the rapidly changing culture of the thirties. Radio dramas were popular and they set the stage for many of our current film ideas. Detectives, crime fighters and science fiction all honed their teeth in the format of radio dramas. Music was appealing to the youth market with big band swing. Sadly during this time people still suffered from the hardships that the depression brought. Still the future looked bright and there was great hope for a better tomorrow.

Hope is something many don't have today because they do not put their faith in the risen Lord Jesus Christ. They feel life is unfair and that people that love the Lord don't have their feet firmly planted in reality. But God is the creator of all. The beauty of nature and the reality of all the wonders of this world. Just because this world isn't the way you think it should be doesn't mean that God doesn't care for all His *creation. Most people I talk to that don't look at life as a positive experience don't have God in their life. They don't have hope and the promise of eternal life.*

Lord, Thank you for making this wonderful world filled with hope and help me be a better caretaker of your creation.

*S*o Jesus answered and said, "were there not ten cleansed? But where are the nine? Were there not any found who returned to give glory to God except this foreigner?" And He said to him, "Arise, go your way. Your faith has made you well." Luke 17:17-19 NKJV

Faith is what you gain when you believe in God the creator of all. Whether it is an issue of blood or a person who has leprosy their faith gives them the opportunity to receive a miraculous healing. Luke relates stories that reinforce this basic idea. In his stories their faith alone provides all that is needed. The determination to seek the Lord, the humbleness to ask for help and the gratitude to give thanks for the healing are the main ideas.

In this modern world of medical advances we forget that God can heal all ills. We can't use our insurance card for this service only through our faith in God do miracles happen. No copay no forms to fill out, just ask God through prayer to provide for you. Many today forget to thank God for what they have already received. Giving thanks for the life we already have is the greatest show of faith. Many have been healed but not all give thanks.

Take time out to read chapter 17 in Luke. Many of these stories are the backbone of popular sermons. Giving thanks is often overlooked because of the of the focus put on faith. We would say that giving thanks is what makes us faithful. Give thanks today for the life you have. It may not be what you had envisioned but with faith in God you have the power to strive toward perfection.

Are you striving toward perfection in you walk with Christ?

God, I know I'm not perfect but help me to be more like your Son every day.

*F*or Ezra had prepared his heart to seek the Law of the Lord, and to do it, and to teach statutes and ordinances in Israel: Ezra 7:10 NKJV

My wife and I often coin new phrases to use in our writings. Repurposed by God is my favorite. This is when a person's life has been changed to have a new and positive direction. Many people that lose a job or retire find new meaning in life as they start to reach out to others in the community. Their wisdom and life experience give them a new and reinvigorated purpose.

We love a good Bible study class and recently found a man that is an expert teacher. Mark teaches because he has the time now that he has retired. Working in the food industry for years he would tell people about the blessing of knowing the Lord as he traveled from store to store. Mark's love of the Old Testament gives him knowledge that can't be found in many classes. The job of a good teacher is to inspire you to repurpose your life. The goal of any class is to gain understanding. The more understanding you have the more wisdom you will gain.

Wisdom allows you to talk with confidence. To study, to live, to teach like Ezra. We have heard many stories of how a great teacher guided someone's life so they could be repurposed. That is what Jesus did, he took twelve men and changed the world, that's real repurposing.

Are you diving into the Bible with new vigor looking to the word to guide your life through troubled times?

Lord give me the power to persevere even when I don't think I can get the job done.

*T*herefore do not cast away your confidence, which has great reward. For you have need of endurance, so that after you have done the will of God you will receive the promise: Hebrews 10:35 NKJV

Jan Karon has a new Mitford novel out called Somewhere Safe with Someone Good. When Jan Karon was close to fifty she read a book that inspired her to begin her writing career. It was Village Diary by Dora Saint, aka Miss Read. This book so inspired her that she left her life in advertising behind and struck out to be an author. She has gone on to write great stories about small town life.

Many today find very little safety from the pressures of the world in the towns were they live. To make your way in life, to strike out on your own can be filled with fear and trembling, as Jan Karon would say. People no matter their age can start a new and purposeful life. They can provide somewhere safe and be a good person to someone who does not have the advantages that so many possess.

As a like minded group of Christians we need to reach out to all people. To be giving and kind. We will all be better served if we think how our actions affect others. Showing God's love is what we can do to make life better for all people. His word is the anchor in the storm. If you want a better world you will have to build one using the word of God.

Are you filled with fear and trembling? Are you ready to make the decisions that will improve your life?

Lord, you are good and have provided safety for me. Help me provide for others so they will know your name.

If someone says, "I love God and hates his brother, he is a liar; for he who does not love his brother whom he has seen, how can he love God who he has not seen? And this commandment we have from Him: that he who loves God must love his brother also. 1 John 5:20

After a long discussion with a homeless man I asked him why he worked so hard to get money for cigarettes. He searched trash cans and ditches for aluminum cans and scrap metal. Then he would walk a couple of miles with his small load of scrap and hopefully have enough for a pack of cigarettes. He told me on a good day he could find enough scrap to get a couple beers.

When your homeless, loneliness can be your biggest problem. For some a cigarette can be your best friend and a beer your only entertainment. Loneliness can be a big problem for those on the street. Rejected by family, looked down on by society and forgotten by most Christians. Luckily in our area people are reaching out to feed and clothe the less fortunate.

Why do homeless people and those who need assistance come to this area? Because there is a group of people here that care about them. The lonely and hungry can find two hot meals within walking distance or within a short drive almost everyday. Food is handed out at local churches along with clothing. The streets are safe and local people are fairly tolerant. For those that can't conform to structured life, or drink and use drugs, life on the streets can make sense.

Are you trying to encourage those that need a hand up with the word of God?

Lord help me find a way to show people the blessing that can be theirs with knowledge from Your word.

When repairing a car or a house, the condition makes it not worth the effort and money that it takes to restore it to original condition. But when it comes to people in need, we can't put a value on their restoration to a purposeful life. Many who were down and out have been helped to regain their place in the society of today. Many have gone on to be leaders and advocates of change and Christian beliefs.

We call this change re-purposing. When someone gets help and goes on to help others in need. These people are like a builder or mechanic who would be knowledgeable of the cost and effort to make the repairs on a house or car. Someone who has used the system for assistance knows what is needed to improve the lives of those who are homeless or living below the standard income levels. Many today seek help for food and living expenses. Sadly few are in a position to move to a higher standard of living.

Standards for the funding of such programs allow only a certain amount of income. For food to be available and to have utility bill reduction, one must fall below an income level. The problem starts with people that show no income and those who's debt consume most of their income. Many people work hard to just be considered poor. This is a disincentive for wage improvement and saving on the part of the person in need. More income means less help and less help means more out of pocket costs. How we can build a better economic base for the less fortunate is a matter of debate.

Are you seeing people that need assistance with their bills or need food? What are your ideas on helping those that don't have the advantages that you have?

Lord, in this land of abundance help us find a way to help those that need help with their bills and provide them a hand up, not a hand out.

We are hard pressed on every side, yet not crushed; we are perplexed, but not in despair. 2 Corinthians 4:8 NKJV

If you have not accepted Jesus Christ as your personal savior you will not have eternal life. The idea of eternal life is what attracts so many to come to know the Lord. Jesus talks of the coming Kingdom of God here on earth. Where all will be restored to the way God had originally planned for it to be. The perfect world where you and God can walk together in the garden he has made for you.

The Bible is full of war, killing and intrigue. These stories explain man's evil nature outside the laws of God. Jesus' message is one that tells mankind to find new purpose in their life on earth as a way of ushering in the coming Kingdom of God. Waiting on his return we have sometimes strayed from his teachings. Let's look toward making this world a better place until his return.

Problems have challenged many churches, but we must look to our ability to persevere, focusing on the tasks at hand. We may be perplexed, but not in despair. As finances become a problem and attendance falls to new lows we as Christians must reach out to all mankind to keep the message of the Risen Lord alive. So many people face challenges today that only we, as like minded Christians can solve. God's love and his forgiveness is what will help bring back those lost sheep that have strayed from the fold.

Are you persevering in troubled times giving a message of forgiveness and love?

Lord, allow me to do Your work to usher in the Kingdom of Heaven.

And Jesus said to him, "Today salvation has come to this house, because he, too, is a son of Abraham. For the Son of Man has come to seek and to save that which is lost." Luke 19:9-10 NKJV

What is faith? It is the belief in a higher power. My higher power is the living Lord Jesus Christ. Faith in God as a force of change is not understood by all people the same way. Not just by region or status. Not just by teaching and practice. Faith creates the life a person lives. From inner city to rural west faith can be the same but your beliefs can vary widely. Those that face problems of poverty and crime may have far different beliefs than those that see promise and success.

We don't judge a man's house by how luxurious it is because our house is quite simple. We look how neat and orderly it is. But ours is not too neat and orderly. This is where belief comes in, many believe God's house is just how they like it. They tell you all about it. It's where they will have a better life and mansions of gold. They will be free from the grips of poverty and discrimination. All pain and suffering will be gone. We could go on for hours.

God's house is just the way He likes it and because it's His house you can't do anything to change it. We all have our vision but that's all it is, our vision. We can change things here. We can eliminate poverty and discrimination. We can eliminate drug and alcohol abuse along with the suffering it causes. God wants us to work on our house and make it the kingdom of God.

Are you working for change by using the word of God? Has the promise of heaven overshadowed the command to love your brother.

Lord, guide me to help those that don't know Your word so they will be spared from the untruths of man's ideas.

*I*t is doubtful that God can use us greatly until He has wounded us deeply. A. W. Tozer

Sometimes there are people that you are not able to help. You don't understand their needs and you don't have the knowledge that is needed to solve their problems. There are plenty of people you can help. Not with money, not with food but with a kind word that comes from your heart. Those people that you can't help can be helped with the word of God. God waits patiently to help those that don't want to help themselves. Where you might be frustrated and lose your patience, God has all the time in the world.

Homeless and alone looking for money those on a quest for the pleasures of man can be a nuisance. Drugs, alcohol and homelessness go hand in hand with a bad economy. Some small towns that never experienced these types of issues are now overwhelmed by an influx of homeless people. Problems begin with how to give a hand up not a hand out. One problem of homelessness is many people are unsympathetic to their plight.

Begging for money, loitering, drug and alcohol use in public all make for a problem that needs to be addressed. Many towns have areas where this behavior is tolerated because it keeps it from spreading to more prosperous business areas. But concentrating the homeless in an area of town does not help the root causes. The sad part is this type of behavior is growing as the areas jobs move away. Reversing the job flight from this area and improving employment opportunities is *important. But it is up to like minded Christians that want to improve this area to get the job done.*

Lord, help us find a way that those in our area will be without financial need. Providing jobs and education for all who want a better future.

*T*o be saved is to do the will of the Father in heaven. That is what Jesus says. You can read that in Matthew 7:21-23. This verse tells that you can prophesy, cast out demons and do miracles and not be saved. Why? Jesus says because they did not do the will of My Father. Read the verse in Matthew that is what it says. You have to do the will of God in heaven not just say you believe in Jesus. Read chapter seven in Matthew and come to your own conclusion.

Many wonder whether they are saved, but are they doing the will of God or practicing the powers of man. Some even use the word of God for personal gain or status. What will happen when they call Lord, Lord. Working toward being more like Christ is all we can do. To read and study, gaining wisdom as we travel the path to salvation. Along our journey we must do the will of God reaching out to those who don't know His name.

Do you have a clear understanding of what being saved involves. Doing the will of God is what Jesus tells us is most important. I would suggest the video by James MacDonald, "Are you saved?" You can agree or disagree but this sermon will help you on your walk with Christ.

Today's world is built on the pleasures of man. Often the word of God is packaged like fast food. Take time and study the Bible. know what you believe is true. Gain the knowledge that is needed to defend your ideas and don't be afraid to admit that you don't know. Honesty and study will help us do the will of God and Jesus tells us that is how we get to heaven, by doing the will of God.

Are you studying the Bible so you can do the will of God? Are you working on your personal relationship with God so you can reach out and help others?

Lord, help me do the will of God and tell people of Your Son.

I have considered my ways and have turned my steps to your statutes. I will hasten and not delay to obey your commands. Though the wicked bind me with ropes, I will not forget your law. At midnight I rise to give you thanks for your righteous laws. I am a friend to all who fear you to all who follow your precepts. The earth is filled with your love, O Lord teach me your decrees. Psalm 119 59-64 NIV

The people around you so often don't have your best interests at heart. I deal with people whose lives are filled with regret. Many ruined their lives in a vain attempt at personal pleasure. Sadly many involved others in their quest of self discovery which usually involved dangerous and irresponsible behavior.

Lack of personal responsibility and a desire to escape the harsh realities of life is frequently discussed as the initiator of many long term problems. Drugs and alcohol use can seem innocent and even attractive, but visit an A.A. or N.A. meeting. You will hear stories that are anything but glamorous.

Many young people feel the need to experiment with drugs as a rite of passage into adulthood. This cycle needs to be broken. I can say I've never met a person whose life was made better through drug or alcohol use. Many young people ask me if I think people benefit from their experiences of drug and alcohol use. I honestly say no I don't see any benefit for anyone involved.

Are you reaching out to help turn people away from drug and alcohol use? Are you working to change our societies glamorous view of the pleasures of man.

Lord, help me change this world so people don't fall victim to drug and alcohol abuse.

I am the Lord, and there is no other, I form the light and create darkness, I make peace and create calamity; I, the Lord, do all these things. Isaiah 45:7 NKJV

Holiday events, family gatherings, travel and shopping can combine into a time of great stress. Many find themselves involved in dredging up old jealousies and disagreements some from childhood. God may not be working in some of your family members lives. Still you need to show them Christian love and present a good example as a testimony of your love for God.

Bad behavior can spoil any gathering, I know this from personal experience. Setting a tone of tolerance and Christian kindness is all important. This time of the year is when we all need to focus on showing love toward all men. Today many people feel that there is very little love in the world and when I look around I have to agree.

Parents at odds with their older children, ex-spouses and children born out of wedlock can all make for awkward family events. When it comes to family gatherings marriage, relationships and children can make things as confusing as this modern world can be. God gives us a clear path to follow but many have strayed from that path. It is up to us as Christians to reaffirm the word of God and inspire people with what He has planned for all our lives.

Are you reaching out during the holidays to give a message of the risen Lord? Have you placed God as the centerpiece of your gathering?

Lord, during this stressful and confusing time of year let me give a message that will guide others to Your word.

This Book of the Law shall not depart from your mouth, but you shall meditate on it day and night, that you may observe to do according to all that is written in it. For then you will make your way prosperous, and then you will have good success. Joshua 1:8 NKJV

God gives us the power to be successful. It may not be the success we have in mind but it will be success. Education, career and family can bring success in the terms of man. Real success is eternal life in heaven. Today many get ahead and benefit financially but are not successful. In their own admission there is a void in their life. Some turn to the things of man to fill that void. Food, sex and alcohol can take control in this search for the feeling of success. The pleasures of man can give us a feeling of power and status. Sadly this quest can be a double- edged sword and end in heartache.

Success is used too freely in the descriptions of our everyday life. The term success in the KJV Bible is only used once. The word success is only used in this above verse, talking about the Book of the Law. The word success can be used for wealth, athletic ability and social status. Today this word has become overused to the point that it describes a brand of non-stick rice. What is success, read the verse above and then make your way prosperous.

Are you striving for the wrong kind of success that are the pleasures of man?

Lord give me true success through the words You have written to guide my life.

*O*nly *be strong and very courageous, that you may observe to do according to all the law which Moses My servant commanded you; do not turn from it to the right hand or the left, that you may prosper wherever you go. Joshua 1:7 NKJV*

So often I make mistakes giving bad advice or misquoting something in the Bible. People that I write for want to know what their being told is correct. I recently wrote that the word success appears only once in the Bible, that is, in the King James Bible and is listed that way in Strong's concordance. In all other translations all bets are off and that's a not a joke. So many that hold to the use of just the King James version would not understand the problem of writing to those that read all sorts of translations.

The problem is man, we want things our way in very neat packages that make sense. But so often there are far ranging ideas that change our perspective. To me success is just getting to know God. To many others God doesn't figure into success in the same way. Many feel they know what God wants in their lives and the lives of others. This is proven out in how people translate the Bible and then interpret that translation. Take time out to read Joshua in a couple different translations and reflect on how they differ.

We all have our view of the world and how God has placed us in this grand adventure. Success is a clear view that many are seeking and never find. God gives us a clear message, it is up to us not to twist that message for our own advancement and profit. Read the verse above in the New

King James and then read the whole first chapter. You will see that God is giving a very clear message to all of us; all we need to do is listen and obey.

Are you listening to God's voice today?

Lord, let me hear clearly the plans you have for my life.

All scripture is given by the inspiration of God, and is profitable for doctrine, for reproof, for correction, for instruction in righteousness: that the man of God may be complete, thoroughly furnished unto all good works. 2 Timothy 3:16 NKJV

Many of us are like large unfurnished house, beautiful on the outside and empty on the inside. That empty feeling in our hearts keeps us from drawing close to God. The bad part is it causes us to be resentful and unforgiving in our dealings with our fellow man.

Forgiveness is a complex thing, I often wonder if God has forgiven the devil for being such a bad angel. I wonder if I can truly forgive my fellow man and whether some day I will know God's grace. As I listen to many speeches about God and forgiveness people that teach these messages have a far different view of life. They are like a furnished houses filled with the word of God. They are forgiving and separate themselves from the what is in it for me mentality.

Today many people don't understand what is involved in forgiving your fellow man. They hold up all sorts of reasons for resentment and hatred toward those that have done them wrong. Money, politics and religion are the hammer that drives the wedge between many a person. Bitterness and resentment is the end result of many disagreements. You have to forgive those that have wronged you, that is the message of Jesus. Look at Matt. 18:21-35.

God gives you a clear message about all things. Forgiveness sometimes gets overlooked. God inspired all the writing in the Bible, every word is the breath of God; it teaches truth and the best part it is profitable. The scriptures equip you for every good work. All of the Bible equips you to change to be like God wants you to be.

Lord, help me be kind and forgiving with my fellow man. Let me be like a furnished house, filled with the word of God.

*B*eloved, do not imitate what is evil, but what is good. He who does evil has not seen God. 3 John 11 NKJV

How do you answer the question where do homeless people come from? Why do people throw their lives away for drugs and alcohol? How can people that have fallen through the cracks in our society be brought back into a normal life style? The real question for many is do you really care about your fellow man?

Today many reach out to those who need help but the problems of the disenfranchised seem to be growing at an alarming rate. As people become older and drugs more prevalent the numbers who need assistance is growing in many areas. Slow economic growth, increasing costs and changing attitudes all impact the amount of help needed in an area. Many cities are having problems providing services for residents let alone helping people that are homeless.

The amount of veterans that need assistance is growing at an alarming rate. The availability of hard drugs is another problem with heroin causing a shocking amount of deaths. Hospitals are impacted by the increasing hard drug abuse. Mental issues, emotional problems and drug use fill our emergency rooms. Today we need to focus on promoting rehabilitation, education and the word of God to help those less fortunate. Work, housing and education is what can turn a life around. How we can provide these things is through our love and the word of God.

Are you trying to help someone who needs the word of God in their life? Are you showing kindness to someone that needs a real friend and a real message?

Lord, help us help those that can't help themselves.

*D*o not be rash with your mouth, and let not your heart utter anything hastily before God. For God is in heaven, and you on earth; therefore let your words be few. For dreams come through activity, and a fool's voice is known by his many words. Ecclesiastes 5:2-3 NKJV

We often need to be brought back to earth. Many times we find ourselves thinking about how important our life is when most of the time we are just going through the motions. We foolishly imagine our life different than it really is self centered and not thankful. We know to put God first but that doesn't always happen.

Many people are flying high with money and success at their backs. All the success in the world and all the riches does not draw you closer to God. Many people are high fliers, talented and successful in every way, but many people never pass on their knowledge and wisdom. The Bible is a book that does just that. It teaches you how to be like Christ. An example of a full person complete in every way. A person that uses their life experiences for the betterment of his fellow man.

Our world has become fast paced and often superficial. Today the world is rapidly changing and for many becoming more complex. The me generation on steroids obsessed with social media is a phrase that has been used as a description of life today. What we as Christians pass on to the next generation is what will form our future world. Take time out of your busy day to lead and guide someone who could use your expertise. Use the word of God to help you improve *lives and provide wisdom that will lead the next generation to a bright and prosperous future in Christ.*

Are you thinking about others and how you can provide knowledge and inspiration for the next generation? Are you showing a young person the skills you have learned?

Lord, let my words help people to reach out to others.

*T*he righteous cry out, and the Lord hears, and delivers them out of all their troubles. The Lord is near to those who have a broken heart, And saves such as have a contrite spirit. Many are the afflictions of the righteous, But the Lord delivers him out of them all. Psalms 35:17-19 NKJV

Untreated depression leads to all sorts of problems. Families who's loved ones suffered from this problem often have stories that don't end well. All that is left is the unhappy ending. That's a line from the song, "What Becomes of the Brokenhearted" the Motown hit by Jimmy Ruffin. For many that are brokenhearted, depression can overtake their lives. Depression ruins many peoples lives in America. A country that has more freedom and opportunity than most places in the world. Yet with all this abundance people are unhappy, depressed and brokenhearted. For many people and their families there can be a happy ending.

Medicine, diet and exercise are all recommended as treatments for depression. Not stigmatizing people for being depressed is one of the best things that has happened in recent years. As Christians we must reach out to those who suffer from depression. The uplifting word of God and a loving Christian family can help those who suffer from depression. Those who do not seek help or don't have caring friends can slip into a dark mood that can lead to drugs, alcohol and even homelessness.

Those that grieve the loss of a loved one need special care. I always recommend attending a grief share group in your area. Having been helped and inspired by going to grief share *meetings myself. I tell all those I meet that suffer grief related depression to take advantage of the wisdom and Christian fellowship at these types of meetings.*

Lord, thank you for making the yoke I carry light and allow me the wisdom to help those who suffer under a heavy load.

*H*e who is unjust let him be unjust still; he who is filthy let him be filthy still; he who is righteous let him be righteous still; he who is holy, let him be holy still. "And behold I am coming quickly and my reward is with Me, to give to everyone according to his work. I am the Alpha and the Omega, and the beginning and the end, the First and the Last." Revelation 22:12-13 NKJV

Some groups and religions believe that you have to work your way up through their organization for you to reach heaven while others cringe at the word work. God has provided for your salvation all you have to do is believe in the death and resurrection of Jesus Christ. After this simple idea of belief in Jesus as savior, many groups want to place all sorts of rules and regulations.

Do they help you be a better Christian? Working together as believers in Christ should be an easy thing, but the regulations and laws that form our brand of religion can form a chasm that can't be bridged. Getting believers in Christ to get together is a difficult task and in some cases impossible. Religious beliefs can cause one group not to be allowed to participate in activities with another group. An old Baptist preacher told me that in Elkins there were two churches one said there is a hell the other said the hell there is.

We can't change people's beliefs or their religions, but we can work together as better Christians to make life better for all. We can provide a message of Christ while not involving ourselves in a debate over our religious beliefs and theology.

How do you receive Christ's rewards? Obey the laws of God. Jesus will give his reward to everyone according to their work.

Are reaching out to all believers in Christ. Giving them a message that you know is true?

Lord help me respect others beliefs, but let me not lose sight of your true word.

The Lord is my shepherd; I shall not want. He makes me lay down in green pastures. He leads me beside the still waters. He restores my soul. He leads me in the paths of righteousness. For his name's sake. Yea, though I walk through the valley of the shadow of death, I will fear no evil; for You are with me; Your rod and staff, they comfort me. Psalm 23:1-4 NKJV

The loss of a loved one can cause a deep depression to come over a person and the holidays only make those feelings worse. Time can be a healing force but for many that sense of loss can affect their relationship with family and friends. To understand your feelings you can turn to the verse above. As I walk through the valley of the shadow of death. That shadow is your memories of those you have lost. It is also how you deal with the idea of your own mortality.

A pastor explained to me that if a truck rushes by you and casts a shadow on you, you weren't hit by the truck. You were just hit by the shadow it cast. Death is like that, a shadow that is cast on our life, it can cause fear and confusion but your still alive. Our life and how we live it is a testament of our faith in God. Traumatic events cause some to lose their faith and others to gain a far greater strength than they thought was possible.

Today many that have lost loved ones are in the shadow of depression and sadness. Some have a feeling of loneliness and sorrow from being without a beloved family member. You have someone who is there for you in your times of sorrow, someone who hears your every word. All you have to do is call out to God and He will hear your plea. He will send a calming spirit to take away your heartache, all you have to do is to sincerely ask.

Because the Lord is your shepherd you shall not want as He restores your soul. You shall not want as He leads you to green pastures on the path of righteousness.

" *The intelligent man is always open to new ideas. In fact he looks for them."* Proverbs 18:15 NLB

A hand up not a hand out is a good idea to help those in need. Education, financial assistance and transportation are needed to secure a steady job. In this area jobs are hard to come by and getting to them is even harder for those with troubled lives.

Working together as a group of like minded Christians we need to encourage economic redevelopment in this area. We must look at public transportation as a way to help people get to work and restore their place in society. Low cost educations, job training and apprenticeships could facilitate change in the employment arena.

The difficult changing landscape for jobs in this area needs a long serious look. Bringing jobs to this county is important for revitalization to gain a foothold. One of the major problems is how assistance is set up and paid to the poor. When a person rings the bell for the Salvation Army the hourly rate he is paid is subtracted from his assistance. If a person who gets V.A. food vouchers and help with their gas bill, such as P.I.P., any money they make may cause them to lose their qualification.

Changing the way wages are paid to short term workers could be beneficial. Incentives for agricultural training and work like having those in need growing food for those that get food stamps may help. Public beautification projects, land management and city cleaning could all be incorporated into financial assistance and skill building projects.

Lord, let those who have the power find the way to help.

*T*he devil, who deceived them, was cast into the lake of fire and brimstone where the beast and the false prophet are. And they will be tormented day and night forever and ever. Revelation 20:10 NKJV

The power of the devil is the weakness of man. Many today talk of being tempted by the devil but are they looking at themselves. God tells us clearly what is right and wrong. We will knowingly do wrong if we feel the end justifies the means. King David is a example of man's reasoning and he pays a great price.

God knows what is in our heart, there is no escaping His power. He wants us to follow His laws and He wants you to reach out to your fellow man in love and kindness. The devil is a word we use for our own disobedience to God's laws through our weakness and temptation, that is our love of power, greed and pleasure.

I hear people preaching about the devil and giving testimonies about being tempted by the devil, but I am not sure that they aren't talking about themselves. Do they know God's laws and his word? Are they truly saved? What would the devil have to offer, nothing is the answer, so why would they be tempted. The reason is because many do not want to follow God's laws and many are worshiping the pleasures of man. For them greed, power and pleasure rule their lives because of their lack of faith in God.

We are working to be like Jesus. If your a Christian that is what is requested of you. Jesus was not tempted by the devil in the wilderness and if your becoming like Jesus you won't *be either. Jesus told the tempter that God was all powerful and nothing he had to offer was of any value. Christians still go on and on about being tempted by the devil. Why don't they know he has nothing to offer? I would say many are still focused on the pleasures of man not the promises of God.*

Lord, You give me the light to see the devil has no power.

A nd they said to one another, *"Did not our heart burn within us while He talked with us on the road, and while He opened the Scriptures to us?" So they rose up that very hour and returned to Jerusalem, and found the eleven and those who were with them gathered together, saying "The Lord has risen and has appeared to Simon!" Luke 24:32-34 NKJV*

When did you first see Jesus? I have only seen representations of Him though some claim to have walked with Him in heaven. The first time I saw a portrait of Him that I could identify with was in a Baptist Church where my wife and I were to be married. We had gone to talk to the pastor about being married in his church. Both of us had been attending for some time and my wife was a member. As we went into his office there on the wall was a portrait of Jesus that looked like Errol Flynn to me. The funny part was the pastor said that everybody said it looked like Errol Flynn.

My mother always talked about Errol Flynn when I was young she had been the film critic for her school paper and had seen all the movies from the late thirties and early forties. As a leading man he played the romantic adventurer, in real life his playboy life style was one of great controversy. Drinking, carousing and womanizing were the words she used to describe his activities. I can dig that, or in modern English I can personally understand the problems he was facing.

Jesus came to earth as a man so we could see something of ourselves in God. What we see is how much we fall short of what God wants for us. We drink and carouse along with a host of other things, but God still loves us. We all see the face of Jesus differently, it is a reflection of our life. Only until the day when we become like Jesus can we see what his face truly looks like.

Lord, Guide my life and form my thoughts to Yours.

" *That you may love the Lord your God, that you may obey His voice, and that you may cling to Him, for He is your life.*" *Deuteronomy 30;20 NKJV*

The temp is eleven below zero and behind a church that we visit people who have no home live in makeshift shelters that they have built. One man lives in an abandoned concrete block gas meter enclosure, a tarp stretched across the door to fight the wind. Many that are homeless can't fit into the structured life we live. I talk to people that are homeless and encourage them to reconcile with their families. We also give a message of turning to the Lord.

It is heartbreaking to see so many people so lost and alone when God is right there to help them. All they have to do is lay down their vices, the drugs, the alcohol, and the lies. Telling God they can't help themselves and asking him to help them make the move to get help and change their life. If you truly want change in your life there are like minded people that can help you get back on track.

Groups like A.A. and N.A. Have people and meetings that can start you on the road to recovery. But your personal relationship with God is all important. Ask God into your heart and lay down your life of drugs, alcohol and lies. With the Spirit of the Lord in your heart you won't look back fondly, on your past life, as you travel down the road to true recovery. Even those that do not want to get off the streets should be treated as one of God's creations deserving of your love and kindness.

Is your church working to fight the homeless problem? Do you support groups and shelters that provide assistance for the homeless?

Lord, Help me reach out to those that live on the streets with Your word in the spirit of love and kindness.

*F*or this reason we also thank God without ceasing, because when you received the word of God which you heard from us, you welcomed it not as the word of men, but as it is in truth, the word of God, which also effectively works in you who believe. Thessalonians 2:13 NKJV

I used to work at a company that hired a lot of temporary workers. When the company became busy they would hire through a temp service and every once and a while one of those people would be hired permanently. Most of the temps that came in had done all sorts of jobs from telemarketing to construction work. A well rounded work experience can make for a better employee and a happier worker. The more work experience the better a person is at solving problems.

Growing in your knowledge and how to present a meaningful message to the unsaved falls into the work related category. This is experience gained when Christians are working with people that don't know the Lord. They increase their knowledge and wisdom through discussion and interaction. Each day during a meaningful conversation a question may come to mind. Usually it's something in the Bible that we did not know or need a better understanding of to make our message clear. We find that reaching out to others is beneficial for both parties.

Reaching out to others is something we should do at every opportunity. At work, shopping or just in casual conversations with friends, a message of helping others should be given. Promoting Christians reaching out to help all people is something Paul talked about in great length. Traveling and *teaching those that did not know the risen Lord gave him more knowledge and wisdom everyday. That is what God wants for us, to improve our minds and help others change. Lord, please put the words of change in my mouth.*

*And when He had taken the five loaves and two fish, He looked up to Heaven, blessed and broke the loaves and gave them to His disciples to set before them; and the two fish He divided among them all. So they all ate and were filled.
Mark 6:41-42 NKJV*

What can you do to go to Heaven? Believe in God and the death and resurrection of Jesus Christ. Believe with all your heart. Many well meaning Christians reach out to others in the hope that they will turn to the word of God. Hoping that others will experience the joy and blessings He bestowed on them. Belief is the foundation of hope. If you do not believe in God then you have no hope of going to Heaven. Non-believers have no hope. No hope of an eternal life in Heaven.

Reaching out with a message of truth is paramount. God wants you to have a personal relationship with him. If you don't believe in God; if you don't believe in the death and resurrection of Jesus Christ how can you believe in Heaven? How can you have hope? How can you go to Heaven if you don't believe it exists. Jesus looked up to Heaven before He performed the miracle of the loaves and fish.

Are you looking up to Heaven? Are you believing with all your heart that God can provide for you? Do you through your belief in the risen Lord have hope?

Lord, give me the strength to have hope and to believe that you will provide for my every need.

*P*eter seeing him, said to Jesus, "But, Lord what about this man." Jesus said to him, "If I will that he remain till I come, what is that to you? You follow me?" John 21:21-22 NKJV

The winters here can be brutal and driving on the highway is a learned skill that some never master. If you get to close to the edge of the road the heavy compacted snow left by the snow plow can pull you off the road into the ditch. Life is like that in so many ways, you first must always pay attention and second you must work on your skills.

Jesus was always trying to train Peter to be a good leader but Peter was like many of us and wanted to do things his way. Many times he would end up in the ditch. Peter says to Jesus about John, "What about this man." The last message Jesus gives to Peter is to not be concerned about what is expected of others. John will do what he will do and you will tend my sheep. You will feed my sheep and you will follow me even if it means you shall die. If John lives till I return so be it.

Today as we read these words many of us have plans that are different than the plan of God. We will find this out when we are in the ditch. Much like Peter when he did his own thing, life didn't work out like he planned. Peter goes on to be a great leader and a driving force of change. He still has some rough edges; Paul makes comments about this in his writings. John goes on to write some of the most influential words ever written that form the ideas about Christ we hold true today.

Are you letting God run your life or are you questioning his word?

Lord, Help me follow Your word so I can do Your work.

*F*or I am your fellow servant, and of your brethren the prophets, and of those who keep the words of this Book. "Worship God." And he said, "Do not seal the words of this prophecy of this book for the time is at hand." Revelation 22:9-10 NKJV

Are you going to Heaven or are you in training for Heaven? Today you have to train for your profession, but are you training for Heaven. Being what you consider a good Christian does not mean God doesn't have the final say. Saved or not saved has the last word for many, but God still has the last word no matter what you say. Your personal relationship with God has everything to do with your eternal future. Faith and dedication to a religion or not, God has the last word. All your hard work and dedication if not focused on your personal relationship with God can cause you to fall short.

I spend time talking with friends that have different views about how they will get to Heaven and for some they don't look at Heaven in the same way as most Christians. We must remember that God has the final say when it comes to your eternal life. If you have worked all your life to be a better Christian you may not have been in training. Many self promote looking for power and position. Others look for fame and recognition as a way to show their closeness to God, but God still has the final say. If you have joined a church to get to Heaven God still has the final say.

I asked a friend of mine to tell me how you get to Heaven, his answer was to truly to believe in God. Sometimes in our *quest for God we become so involved in religion that we put our personal relationship with God second. And sometimes we become so fixated on what we think God wants in our life we put our religion first. It is your personal relationship with God that makes you a true Christian; why, because God has the final say.*

Lord, God allow me to follow you as your servant.

For a good tree does not bear bad fruit, nor does a bad tree bear good fruit. For every tree is known by its own fruit. Luke 6:44 NKJV

Are we truly thankful for the life we have? Many are disappointed at the path they have taken for themselves and try to place the blame on others or on circumstance. Many don't realize how fortunate their life has been. They become dissatisfied and bitter about how their lives have panned out over time. Panned out is a gold mining term used when separating gold ore from the river gravel. When there is no more wealth to be found in a creek or steam it is panned out.

Low hanging fruit is a similar phrase, the taking of an easy harvest and moving on looking for more abundance. People often take the easy path to prosperity. They choose the low hanging fruit and soon that endeavor doesn't pan out. In Christianity reaching out to family and friends can be considered low hanging fruit. To reach out to people who have no knowledge of the word of God can be a far more challenging task.

As Christians we all need to take on that challenge reaching out to those that don't know the word of God or have had experiences with religion that have drove them from faith and worship. The Lord promises you mansions of gold in heaven all you have to do is obey his word. We all need to go out and tell the good news to all that will listen.

Are you reaching only for the low hanging fruit? Are you looking for the gold that can only be found with using the word of God?

Lord, help me bear good fruit and reach out to those that have not heard the word of God.

*C*oming to Him as to a living stone, rejected by men, but chosen by God and precious, you also, as living stones, are being built up a spiritual house, a holy priesthood, to offer up spiritual sacrifices acceptable to God through Jesus Christ. 1 Peter 2:4-5 NKJV

Kindness abounds at Christmas, from opening doors to giving money, people are on their best behavior. This is the attitude we should have everyday the attitude of gratitude. God has provided us with the ability to love and show kindness. All we have to do is make it the foundation of our Christian life. This foundation is made of living stones. Kind and caring people that are driven by their love of God to care about their fellow man.

Jesus is the foundation, the living stone which all good is built on. Our life must be focused on the completion of the spiritual house being built for us by God. For those who have had troubled lives this verse makes it clear what we have to do to change our life. We have to come to Jesus as the living stone. A foundation that will give us strength. Jesus who was chosen as the foundation stone, but was rejected by man. He gave His life for us, so we as believers in Jesus or living stone as Peter says, are now being built up a spiritual house.

Jesus was born so we could have a good foundation and a spirit-filled life. If you are calling out in the darkness Jesus is the light. Today many have no foundation in their life. If you want real change turn to the living stone that is the foundation of all mankind, Jesus Christ.

Lord, help me build the foundation of my spiritual house with the living stones of those who love Christ.

*F*or assuredly, I say to you, whoever says to this mountain, "Be removed and cast into the sea," and does not doubt in his heart, but believes that those things he says will be done, he will have whatever he says. Mark 11:23 NKJV

There is a common saying about not always seeing the negatives in life. You need to focus on the doughnut not the hole. The feeling of emptiness can be like a heavy weight on your shoulders. The word of God can fill that void and bring light into your life. But for many a dark and gloomy cloud continually blocks out the sun. Reading the Bible and attending a church can provide the ladder to climb out of the gloomy abyss of depression.

Young people that don't get a strong message of self worth and mentoring that promotes personal responsibility can fall under this cloud. Young people today may feel that they are limited on the opportunities for success. Educational costs and job availability make the world a scary place for these young people.

Seeing no profit in personal growth and education, a bleak vision of the future has crept into many young people's outlook of life. When we were young the future was so bright we had to wear shades. Today joblessness and drugs have distorted young people's dreams of the future. How we work together to solve this problem will directly impact our next generation.

We are focused on teaching through the word of God. Education and motivation by skilled caring people is needed whether they give a Christian message or not. We find that *if there is a void in a person's life the Word of God helps fill that emptiness. The one thing we all need to focus on is to help our young people have opportunities and education that provide for a secure future.*

Lord, open the eyes of the young people I meet to hear your word and make their lives fruitful.

A nd the King will answer and say to them, Assuredly, I say to you, inasmuch as you did it to one of the least of these My brethren, You did it to Me. Matthew 25:40 NKJV

Many wish for an easier path, but not for a stronger pair of shoes. Today there is a mindset that people should be provided for even if they don't want to provide for themselves. I have actually had misguided people tell me that jail provides what they need, two hots and a cot.

How hard we work when no one is looking is who we really are. Whether talking to young people or those that have fallen on hard times a message of self reliance is important. Even with the large amounts of assistance from religious and private organizations we all must work hard to provide for ourselves. Many who seek assistance don't realize all the effort that goes into providing help for needy families. Food, free hot meals, clothing and financial help requires hard work, time and effort; many times thanks to volunteers.

Those that have placed themselves on the front line of service to their fellow man will receive their reward in Heaven. Those that use the system should look at themselves to see how they can help themselves and others. God wants us to reach out to others if only to show kindness. Jesus says those that have reached out to the lowliest person have reached out to Him.

Are you supporting agencies that reach out to the disadvantaged? Are you giving your time and money to help solve the problem of people in need?

Lord, thank you for all those that have helped me be a better person.

*H*ow can a young man keep his way pure? By living according to your word. I seek you with all my heart; do not let me stray from your commands. Psalm 119:9-10 NIV

A very interesting man who runs the mentoring program at the Salvation Army told me many young men feel that they will be incarcerated at some time in their life. Life in this area does not offer the financial opportunities that it does in some more prosperous locales. This lack of opportunity should not promote criminal behavior, but sadly it does.

Why would a young man through his actions want to trade his freedom for time spent in a jail cell. That is a question that needs to be answered. Why would someone think their life would someday be limited by the iron bars of a jail. For these young men, their dreams may not have been replaced with the interest and determination of young adulthood. Dreams replaced with thoughts of a job, higher education, travel and adventure. For them the world may seem to offer none of these things.

This depressed idea of the world may be creeping into the minds of many youth in America today. When your young, your hope should be high; your ambition strong. The world is a competitive place and people that find happiness and success worked hard for those things. The question is why aren't more people like the man at the Salvation Army focusing their lives on helping youth.

Life doesn't always work out like you planned. Our dreams change as we get older. Some set the bar to high and *don't attain their dreams. Sadly many youth set the bar so low that they have no dreams and no ambition to excel. God's word can fill the void that has taken their hope away.*

Lord, help us all to take the road less traveled and reach out to those that others will not help.

" *I am the good Shepherd. The good shepherd gives his life for His sheep. John 10:11 NKJV*

Jesus talks about being a good shepherd and how the sheep know His voice. We go to different churches and we listen to many sermons on a variety of subjects to aid in our writing. When you hear an inspirational message you can't help but think about the message in Psalm 23. A young pastor was talking about this Psalm while explaining about sheep and how a shepherd cared for them. I couldn't help but think how he was being a good shepherd. Leading and guiding those eager to know the word of God.

Many who preach the word have a strong life changing effect on many who hear them. How those in the audience respond and how they apply the message is what is important. Some put it to work and others put it on a shelf. Today many are in need of an inspirational message to help them go forward to help those that don't know the word of God. Inspiration from the word of God to help those that have lost their way is preached to the flocks of lost sheep all over this world.

Finding a church that gives a message that motivates you to reach out to others is a blessing. Learning the word of God and coming to know the Lord through prayer is what a good shepherd can help you achieve. A good shepherd protects you from false teachers and those that want you to fail.

Is your pastor a good shepherd? Are you being a good shepherd to those that need your help? Is your life focused on helping others and gaining a personal relationship with God through prayer?

Lord, I hear your voice and I know You are the Good Shepherd. Guide me to follow your word.

*H*e that hath not given forth upon usury, neither hath taken any increase, that hath withdrawn his hand from iniquity, hath executed true judgment between man and man. Hath walked in statues, and hath kept my judgments, to deal truly; he is just, he shall surely live, saith the Lord God. Ezekiel 18:8-9 KJV

Reading and studying the Bible can cause us to look at things through a different lens. Studying the Old Testament can give us a different view of the parables of Jesus. This idea came to me while listening to a sermon about the talents. I began thinking the master was dishonest, a hard man and shouldn't profit from his wrong doings nor should his servants participate.

He who is first will be last and the poor will be rich in the coming kingdom of heaven is a message in the words of Jesus. But he quotes the Old Testament when challenged by the devil in the wilderness and at death from the cross. The Old Testament stresses the idea that fellow Jews should not be charged interest and to do good you should not profit from the sale of food or the lending of goods. This makes the story of the talents appear to have a different message than what is generally preached. Most will disagree but you will know why through your study.

Read the verse for yourself, usury is interest. The master can be seen as a dishonest man reaping where he does not sow. Servants are expected to lend money for profit which is against the commands of God. The servant entrusted with the least may have been entrusted with the most, obeying God's *commands as stated in Exodus, Deuteronomy, Leviticus and Ezekiel. Read what the Bible says about interest and then read the story of the talents, it will make it a little more interesting. Are you studying the Bible so you can gain knowledge and wisdom? Don't be afraid to study some of the more difficult books like Deuteronomy or Ezekiel.*

Lord, help me to understand your word.

*V*erily I say unto you, Among them that are born of a woman there hath not risen a greater than John the Baptist; notwithstanding, he that is least in the kingdom of heaven is greater than he. And from the days of John the Baptist until now the kingdom of heaven suffereth violence and the violent take it by force. Matthew 11:11-12 KJV

The troubled world of today is the same as the troubled world of Jesus' time. Look what happens to John the Baptist. Jesus answers the disciples when they ask, "Why then do the scribes say that Elijah must come first?" Jesus answered and said to them, "Elijah is coming first and will restore all things. But I say to you Elijah has come already and they did not know him but did to him whatever they wished. Likewise the Son of Man is also about to suffer at their hands. Then the disciples understood that He spoke to them of John the Baptist.

Today many try in faith to change man's mind but the word of God is all we need. Communication, is most important. Just telling people about the better life they can have through God's word. Perseverance, to keep encouraging during tough times. Conviction, to have an unwavering faith in God and to do his work as a true servant. This is what is needed to bear fruit. We are told all Christians will face troubles and persecution of some sort. It is our duty to persevere. To communicate to those that don't know the Lord with a conviction that shows our true faith. Doing this is what both Paul and Jesus tell us produces good fruit.

Are you telling others about God's love and his promise of salvation?

Lord, help me communicate with conviction and persevere so I can bear good fruit that others will come to know your name.

That ye might walk worthy of the Lord unto all pleasing, being fruitful in every good work, and increasing in the knowledge of God. Colossians 1:10 KJV

When we read this verse about our Christian walk we want to view that through the eyes of Jesus to truly understand. To be more like Jesus is what we strive for. Watching James MacDonald, "Are you saved?," made me see what causes me so many problems. I am in the process of being saved. I will not truly be saved until I am like Christ. We as Christians all say we want to be Christ like but many including myself fall short. Working daily to improve our Christian walk is what is needed. You are either in the process of being saved or in the process of not being saved, you'll know when you get to Heaven.

Conversations with people that strongly hold Christian beliefs can be a double edged sword. Some inspire me to be better and some make me question why I have sought this path. To me being saved is an ongoing process. To love the Lord more each day to have an overflowing of the spirit that reaches out to those that don't know the Lord. Yet many proceed on with the longings of man's mind instead the mind of Christ.

Paul tells us that we must walk in a manner worthy to the Lord, to please Him in all respects, bearing fruit in every good work and increasing in the knowledge of God.

Are you working toward being more like Christ and are you reaching out to those that are not receiving God's word.

Lord give me the wisdom to help solve the problems we face today. And allow me to work toward changing people through your word.

*N*ot everyone who says to me Lord, Lord, will enter into the kingdom of heaven; but he who does the will of My Father who is in heaven. "Many will say to Me on that day' Lord, Lord, did we not prophesy in Your name and in Your name cast out demons, and in Your name perform miracles?" And then I will declare to them, depart from me, you who practice lawlessness. Matthew 7:21-23 NAS*

Falling away or not bearing good fruit is used as a description of faith and belief in the Bible. Churches have people that sit in the seats every Sunday that are in the process of falling away. They are the tares in the wheat or the seed that did not produce a good root.

To bear fruit is what makes you saved. Matthew tells a story that explains what it takes to be saved. Jesus teaches the disciples the of parable of the sower. This story is told then explained to his disciples so they are clear about the meaning. Your continuing faith and actions are what achieves salvation.

Today the concept of being saved is viewed differently from pulpit to pulpit. Many who sit in the pew don't really have a sound concept of what is meant by the term being saved. The bad part is that when you ask people if they are saved they tell you what happened when they were saved. For many they believe they are saved but have a hard time explaining what that involves beyond saying a prayer. Do these people bear fruit and do they persevere. Those would be questions we could ask ourselves.

Do we love God more everyday? Do we reach out to those that have fallen away? If not are we saved?

Lord, Your message is simple. Help me do Your work with a message that is simple and easy to understand.

*N*ow all things are of God, who has reconciled us to Himself through Jesus Christ, and has given us the ministry of reconciliation, that is, that God was in Christ reconciling the world to Himself, not imputing their trespasses to them, and has committed to us the word of reconciliation. 2 Corinthians 5:18-19 NKJV

Family and friendship is something many don't have and others take for granted. For those that are lonely and alone, God is the friend they need. The strong guiding force that can bring about change is His word. Each day we encounter people that could use a kind word or an uplifting message.

A young man came by our church one day while I was talking to a couple of guys that have been homeless on and off for years. He asked the pastor for food and money. He told him how he had been homeless for almost thirty days. I gave him a sobering message that there isn't much help in this area and that he should look towards friends and family for help. Reaching out to people in A. A and church outreach services for the needy can also be a good start. Asking God to help is really what is needed.

For those now facing life on the streets they need to take a thorough self examination of their personal responsibility and motivation. When you give a strong message of self-reliance you will help them see needs they can address. Help many times involves reconciling with family for a second chance. But complex problems like drug abuse can be at the root of many peoples trouble of not having a stable home. Breaking the chains of drugs and alcohol comes first. Then turning to God to lead and guide you is as important as personal motivation for a better life.

Lord, help me break the chains that cause the loneliness of life on the streets. Please help me motivate and guide those who have no home to have a better life in Your word.

A nd the Lord said to Himself: "never again will I doom the earth because of man, since the devising of man's mind are evil from his youth; nor will I ever again destroy every living being, as I have done." Genesis 8:21 JSB

A man asked me where do all the homeless people come from and why do they come here. He said, "There seems to be very little opportunity for a person in this area." People of equal status tend to be drawn together, that includes homeless. People without jobs, transportation and housing tend to congregate in areas where others face the same plight. The real question is why do we have so many disadvantaged people in the first place.

Laws, jobs and education all play a part and can be the basis for many a lively argument. To fix this problem takes a change of attitude. A hand up not a hand out. This is where the problem begins as program after program tries their luck at solving the plight of the homeless. A large percentage can be helped with assistance; some with education and some with rehabilitation. But for many life on the street is the freedom they seek. Freedom's just another word for nothing left to lose and you got nothing if you ain't free. That old song has stuck in my mind for years. Talking to many people that are disadvantaged, they don't understand that personal freedom is what leads them to have a troubled life. God has created man with the power to do just about anything. But God want's us to want the best for ourselves. To be honest, responsible, kind and caring. These are the building blocks of an improved life. A life that follows the word of God.

Are you thinking about the plight of others and what you could do to help them? Are you thinking how you can improve your walk with God.

Lord, help me help others to have a better life through Your word.

*B*ut Reuben heard it, and he delivered him out of their hands, and said "let us not kill him." And Reuben said to them, "Shed no blood, but cast him into this pit which is in the wilderness, and do not lay a hand on him." that he might deliver him out of their hands and bring him back to his father. Genesis 37:21-22 NKJV

When we read Genesis we see a story of Jacob and his sons that will lead to the Laws of Moses. Reuben (behold a son) the first born son and Joseph (increase) the youngest. This idea of first born and youngest are symbolic. The actions of Reuben shows the loving hand of God that will some 430 years later give the Law to Moses. By this act of caring Reuben sets this story in motion. The phrase so he can be brought back to his father is important. The risk of killing his brother was to great for Reuben. The reward was the future nation of Israel.

God works slowly to make the decendant's of Abraham into a loyal group that will follow Moses into the desert. Joseph never lost sight of that God, the God of his father. Joseph's bones are taken in the exodus back to be buried in the land promised to Abraham by God. Risk does not exist just reward when it comes to having God in your life. You know through the stories in the Bible that God is working to reward us. Even in the toughest times our reward is made clear in the Old Testament.

Are you thinking about God's infinite wisdom? Are you thinking about risk and reward as you go about your Christian walk with God?

Lord, thank you. You have made the risks few and the rewards many through your love for me.

A nd which of you, having a servant plowing or tending sheep, will say to him when he has come in from the field, "Come at once and eat?" But will he not rather say to him, "Prepare something for my supper, and gird yourself and serve me till I have eaten and drunk, and after you will eat and drink?" Does he thank the servant because, because he did the things that were commanded him? I think not. So likewise you, when you are commanded, say, "We are unprofitable servants. We have done what was our duty to do." Luke 17:7-10 NKJV

This verse appears just after the apostles say to the Lord increase our faith. Faith and doing what is required is the message. Jesus tells us over and over again. To be more, to love more, to help more; to care more. To do more than you are commanded to do. To truly have the faith of the mustard seed.

During our weekly Bible study as we talked about David this verse just came to my mind. David wanted more for all people and wanted to show more love to God. David loved God and wasn't afraid to show it. David was truly God's servant.

This verse was the last thing I shared with our pastor, he died a few days later. He was truly God's servant reaching out to many in need. His personal concern was what made him more than a servant. I would say he had the faith of a mustard seed and he would spend hours trying to encourage those that didn't. Like David in the Bible our pastor truly loved God and wanted to share that with all people. It wasn't *his duty it was his pleasure to help and inspire others so they could profit from the word of God.*

Are you reaching out to lead and inspire using the word of God? Is it a pleasure for you or is it a duty?

Lord, help me to be a better servant and to do more than is required of me.

*S*o He said to them, *"You will indeed drink my cup and be baptized with the baptism that I am baptized with; but to sit on My right hand and My left is not mine to give, but it is for those whom it is prepared by My Father."* Matthew 20:23 NKJV

The story of the workers in the vineyard is used in churches over and over again to tell you that a new Christian will receive the same blessing as the long time believer. The dialog with Jesus and Peter just before this parable enlightens us about what the disciples questions may have been. But the story after really cements the parables message.

So often we have a bobblehead mentality. We nod in agreement to something we don't fully understand. Peter says, See we have left all and followed you. Therefore what shall we have? Peter followed Jesus and what did he expect would happen? Jesus tells him because he has left all those worldly things he would receive a hundredfold, and inherit eternal life. Does he truly understand that he would be required to die for his beliefs.

Beliefs is the key word. Many that are Christians do not have a firm understanding of what is required of them and how they can achieve a personal relationship with God. Use prayer and Bible study to help your growth as a Christian. The Holy Spirit will help you understand what God has planned for you.

Are you reaching out to others or complaining that your not getting your fair share? The Son of Man did *not come to be served but to serve, and give His life as a ransom for many.*

Lord, help me understand, I know that many are called, but few are chosen, let me be one of the chosen few.

N *ow then we are ambassadors for Christ, as though God were pleading through us: we implore you on Christ's behalf to be reconciled to God. For He made Him who knew no sin to be sin for us, that we might become the righteousness of God in Him. 2 Corinthians 5:20-21 NKJV*

For years now a man comes to my house and witnesses to me leaving his groups literature for me to read. I read it and find most of it quite interesting. I give him my writings knowing that his religion does not allow him to read my material or any that isn't authorized by his group. Sometimes he brings his wife or another member of his group. I would like to have him for a friend, he is smart and interesting and has a great desire to know God. Sadly he is not supposed to socialize with people that are not of his religious organization.

That is the problem, I feel he doesn't personally know God because he only knows God through this organization. He can't understand my feelings about God because I'm not part of his organization. Only when I have become a member of his religion can he then understand my feelings about God. He's well meaning and dedicated but that is not a personal relationship with God. God has the final say not a religious organization no matter how well meaning it is. God first, religion second would be the simplest explanation for me.

My wife and I talk to all people and we write a message to all people. We tell people about God and about the life they can have through their faith in the death and resurrection of Jesus Christ. We also give a strong message against drugs, alcohol and dishonesty. God knows the words I have written on this page and I can only hope my friend will read them and come to his own conclusion. To be an ambassador for Christ is more important than getting people to join your organization.

*F*or I know the plans I have for you, declares the Lord, plans for welfare and not for evil, to give you a future and a hope. Jeremiah 29:11 ESV

Depression is a problem that can be a silent killer. It can be a stumbling block to a successful life and drive a wedge in a marriage. Those working to overcome depression may find a renewed strength in themselves. An inspired strength that molds a new and vibrant outlook on what life holds in-store for them. For many that have suffered under this crushing weight they emerge from this darkness to be a beacon of light for those that still suffer.

Many who turned away from drugs and alcohol say that their depression was made worse by substance abuse. Sadly many originally turned to self medication as a relief from this problem. Over time and with the help of others these people realized that God loved them and that they were precious in His eyes. God wants the best for you and through His word you will come to know the calming power of the Holy Spirit.

Those that have suffered from depression are well served to reach out to those who are now experiencing the heavy burden of this condition. People who have escaped the deep abyss of depression can strengthen themselves while encouraging others to break the chains of this feeling of despair. Recovery involves helping others whether it is depression or drug and alcohol abuse. There is no greater service than reaching out to those in need of your wisdom and knowledge.

Are you helping someone deal with their depression?

Lord, show me the straight path to lead and guide those that have fallen victim to problems I once faced.

*B*ut seek ye first the kingdom of God and his righteousness; and all these things shall be added unto you. Matthew 6:33 KJV

It wasn't until just a few years ago when we started writing a Christian message of encouraging outreach and generosity that I found out my message was flawed. Some didn't like a verse unless it was quoted from the King James Bible. Many others didn't understand how the verse related to the story because it was quoted from the King James Bible.

We encourage you to view problems that you may not usually think about in a different light. Like Acts 17:11-12 says study and decide for yourself. Sadly some will refute this statement, but you still have to come to your own conclusion. My way or the highway is the message of some who will only use the King James Bible. To me that puts you first not God. Others look down on those that allow that type of thinking. That can cause us to be judgmental and get in the way of what God wants for a person. The my way or the highway view knows no denomination. We tell people all we're doing is trying to get people to turn away from the pleasures of man and turn to the word of God.

The pleasures of man are drugs, alcohol and promiscuous sex. That is what we try to write against. We promote a message of people turning to the word of God for a meaningful life. We want you to have a clear understanding of God's word. We read different Bibles translations and listen to dozens of sermons in the attempt of gleaning knowledge and wisdom.

Are you reading the Bible or listening to what people tell you about it's message? Are you studying with a group to gain knowledge and wisdom? Are you praying to God for guidance?

Lord, allow me to give the clear message that will help others and myself know Your word is true

*H*e who has pity on the poor lends to the Lord, And he will pay back what he has given. Proverbs 19:17 NKJV

When involved with helping others and guiding people to Christ many face problems that are right in their own families. Mental illness, depression and physical problems may stress a family but make them a stronger family unit. These problems are not a hurdle for many but an inspiration. Those who work through difficult problems can provide guidance and instruction for those that want to reach out to those in need. Past problems give us a foundation that bolsters us; to provide strength to those that may not be prepared to handle these difficult challenges.

This complex world we live in today requires a skilled administrator and dedicated servants to provide help for those in need. At a church we attend a young woman took on the task of helping with safe housing for the homeless at area churches. Her skills as an administrator and an organizer made the task a pleasure for all involved. People were helped because many volunteered to provide for those in need. Today many are taking on the challenge of helping the homeless. This makes people more aware of this growing problem and provides a working knowledge of what is needed to bring attention to this ongoing effort.

Those who are homeless, alone and confused need skilled people to get them back on track. Jobs, education and child care are all needed. But what is needed most is people who can provide the change that improves peoples lives. Many

whom have faced similar problems are now leading the way. Working toward solving the root cause of homelessness is a daunting task but one that is well worth our time and money.

Lord, help us change this world so there is a home for all who want one.

*T*ake my yoke upon you and learn from Me, for I am gentle and lowly in heart, and you will find rest for your souls. For My yoke is easy and My burden light. Matthew 11:29-30 NKJV

Talking to someone who wants to change but does not realize what is the root cause of their problem can be a daunting task. For those at a low point self examination is important, but asking God for help is the only way to change. What we say is, "Your own pride has pressed you down as low as you think you can go, but still you will not get on your knees to ask God for his help." God has been there all the time but you have tried to do it all yourself.

Alcohol and drugs rule your life and your pride makes you feel your still in control. You blame your problems on others and say that it is bad luck when things go wrong. Personal responsibility is just an occasional thought that is motivated by the wrong you have done to others. You disappoint yourself, but you know you have the ability to be so much more. What overpowers you is your own weakness and desire for pleasure. You call out for help to your fellow man, but you do not turn your eyes to God. You may be enslaved to alcohol or drugs but, with faith in God you have the power to break the chains and free yourself.

There is power in the name of Jesus, to break every chain. To break those chains get down on your knees and ask God to save you from yourself. Ask Him to come into your heart and give you the power to stop blaming others for your problems. Ask Him to break the chains that bind you. Ask Him to give *you the power to turn back from the path you are on today, laying down all the burdens you carry. Become a new person in Christ and follow Him.*

Are you ready to break your chains? Are you sick of trying to do it alone? Get on your knees and ask God into your heart today.

Lord, thank you for providing the power that will break the chains that have caused me so much pain.

Printed in the United States
By Bookmasters